Henry Field

**Among the holy hills**

Henry Field

**Among the holy hills**

ISBN/EAN: 9783337282806

Printed in Europe, USA, Canada, Australia, Japan

Cover: Foto ©Andreas Hilbeck / pixelio.de

More available books at **www.hansebooks.com**

# AMONG THE HOLY HILLS

BY HENRY M. FIELD, D.D.

AUTHOR OF "FROM THE LAKES OF KILLARNEY TO THE GOLDEN HORN,"
"FROM EGYPT TO JAPAN," AND "ON THE DESERT."

NEW YORK
CHARLES SCRIBNER'S SONS
1884

To Mark Hopkins, D.D., LL.D.,

PHILOSOPHER AND TEACHER, GUIDE AND FRIEND,

THESE PAGES ARE INSCRIBED

IN LOVING AND GRATEFUL REMEMBRANCE OF

THE LESSONS OF WISDOM FROM HIS LIPS

LONG YEARS AGO.

# PREFACE.

That so many have been over the ground before, is no reason why the latest comer should not bring home a handful of wild flowers from Palestine. There is enough for all : let each one gather what he will. He who is tempted and led on by these lighter attractions, may find something more and better, as nature leads up to life, and a small mountain country appears as the scene of a great history, and the cradle of a religion. The beauty of nature comes and goes ; it changes with the seasons, with the early and the latter rains ; but the charm of sacred association does not fade with the falling leaf or the departing year. The interest of this above all other lands, is that here was spent the most wonderful life that ever was lived on the earth. To know that life, we would trace it from its beginning, among its native hills. Such a purpose has given direction to the present journey, which follows closely in the footsteps of our Lord, not merely in the streets of Jerusalem, but through Samaria and Galilee, along the lake shore and on the mountain side. Studying the history amid the scenes in which it transpired, it is a constant surprise and delight to see how the narrative fits into the very landscape, and is reflected in it, as trees on the bank of a river are reflected in its bosom. To give freshness to the scene, is to give reality to the event ; faith comes by sight, and as sight grows clearer, faith grows stronger. And so at every step the sacred story becomes more real and more true.

If the descriptions in these pages often digress into reflections, the writer cannot help it : he must speak of that which is uppermost in his thoughts. One presence is everywhere, and we walk in its light. At the same time he has tried not to moralize too much ; but to enliven his soberness with narrative and incident, so that the journey may not seem long, and that whoever keeps him company may not grow weary by the way. Thus riding side by side among the holy hills, we may pass the time not unpleasantly, and gain what is, after all, the best fruit of travel—some real knowledge, a clearer understanding, and a stronger faith.\

# CONTENTS.

# AMONG THE HOLY HILLS.

## CHAPTER I.

### ROUND THE WALLS—THE TOWERS AND BULWARKS.

We had come up to Jerusalem at the time of the Passover. The city was filled with pilgrims; there was the stir and sound of moving to and fro, the buzz and hum of a multitude, such as might have been heard two thousand years ago, when the tribes came up to the solemn feasts. And yet—it was not the Jerusalem of my dreams! I had looked for a city that even in hoary age had some remains of its former magnificence. I had looked also for something that should remind me of the ancient people and the ancient worship—venerable rabbis, with long gray beards and flowing robes, chanting the Psalms of David. But I found little to admire either in the city or its inhabitants. The city is indeed picturesque in situation, standing on its mountain height; and when seen from a distance, with its walls and towers, its appearance is very striking. This rouses the traveller, as he approaches it, to an attitude of expectation, from which he is rudely awakened as he enters within the walls, where the first impression is disappointing, and even painful. It has neither the beauty of a modern city, nor the sombre stateliness of an ancient one. In its interior it has all the unsightly features of an Oriental

town—narrow streets, in which there is no distinction of
the roadway for beasts of burden and the path for human
feet, but men and women are jostled and crowded to the
wall by horses and asses and camels. As the traveller picks
his way over the rough stones, through the deep mire, while
every open door that permits a glance within uncovers a
picture of squalid wretchedness, he feels indeed that this
is not "Jerusalem the Golden."

So wide is the gulf between the Jerusalem that now is
and that which we have had in our imaginings, that many
prefer not to visit it lest the painful sight should disturb
their devout meditations. Mr. Spurgeon, whom I met at
Mentone on my way to the East, expressed a positive reluctance to making a pilgrimage to the Holy Land. He
seemed to fear that the sight of so much that was far from
sacred, would jar painfully on his cherished impressions of
the land where our Saviour lived and died. Such apprehensions would dissuade a traveller from going to Jerusalem, and even if he had been there, would almost discourage
him from attempting to describe it. Possibly we may find
something of a different character. Let us see. |

Jerusalem is a city set on a hill, or rather an elevated
plateau, half a mile above the level of the Mediterranean,
and so cut off by deep ravines from the surrounding country, that it is like a bold headland jutting into the sea, and
joined to the mainland only on its northwestern side. This
neck of land is not very large to be the site of a capital—
only about a thousand acres in all, and to this must be
confined the city that is built upon it. "Jerusalem is
builded as a city that is compact together." It is "compact" because it has no room to expand. In the days of
its prosperity the whole plateau was densely populated.
In the time of Christ the walls were a little more than four
miles in extent; they are now but two and a half. But if

the city be of so limited extent, so much the easier to en-
compass it on every side, and take in its proportions, and
define its character.   ·

To get a general impression of Jerusalem, there is but
one way: "Walk about Zion, and go round about her."
This direction we have obeyed literally, making the circuit
of the city without and within, and going round on the top
of the walls.   Dr. Post of Beirut, who was my companion
on the Desert, and up to the gates of Jerusalem, kindly
offered to be my guide through the streets of the holy
city. /

Our first excursion was outside the walls, and the first
natural feature of the environs we explored, was the Valley
of Hinnom!   This was beginning low enough by a descent
into Gehenna!   Going out by the Jaffa Gate, we turned
to the left and descended the slope, verging away to the
opposite side of the valley, so that we might stand "over
against the city," at a sufficient distance to obtain a general view.   Here we stood facing Mount Zion, its bold
height rising directly before us.   It is a very ancient part
of Jerusalem, for though it bears the name of the City
of David, it was a city, a fortified town or castle, long
before David was born.   Four hundred years after Joshua
crossed the Jordan, and the tribes were settled in different
parts of Canaan, Jerusalem was still held by the Jebusites,
who driven from the valleys, retreated to this mountain
fastness, from which they defied the Hebrew invaders.
The capture of this stronghold was the great military
achievement of Joab, after which David transferred his
seat of government from Hebron to Jerusalem.   A little
below the brow of yonder hill is still pointed out a wall
that is supposed to have been built by the Jebusites, and
close within the wall are old cisterns for securing rain
water, which supplied the garrison. /

Descending into the valley, we are carried back to a point in history still more remote, when this deep yet wide space—like the Campus Martius at Rome—was the scene of feasts and games and of an idolatrous festival which was a carnival of superstition and ferocity, for here the Canaanites celebrated the worship of Moloch by human sacrifices — causing their sons and daughters to pass through the fire. With such associations it is not strange that the Valley of Hinnom had an evil name, as of a place accursed. When the Israelites became masters of Jerusalem, it was made a receptacle for the offal of the city which was cast forth to be burned, so that, as its smoke was continually ascending, it was not an unfit type of the place of torment. Looking down upon it is the Hill of Evil Counsel, on which stood, according to tradition, the house of Caiaphas, to which Judas came to offer the betrayal of Christ. Thus the very air seemed to whisper of treachery and blood. At the present day the valley speaks not of crime so much as of misery, for it is one of the places near Jerusalem where lepers sit by the wayside begging, the most wretched objects ever seen in human form, with bodies dying inch by inch and dropping away, while they stretch out their mutilated hands for alms. |

Leaving the sulphurous atmosphere which may easily be imagined to float over the Valley of Hinnom, as if its fires were still burning, we pass farther round the base of Zion, and come suddenly upon a fountain of bright and sparkling water. This is Siloam, gushing out of the rock at the foot of the Hill of Ophel, which was once included within the walls. The spring flows in such volume as to fill a large "Pool," which supplies the village of Siloam, and to which the women come with their pitchers, and even wash their clothes by the side of the spacious reservoir. Beyond this Pool of Siloam is another spring called

St. Mary's Well, which is fed from the same source, exploration having shown them to be connected, although the distance under the rock is a third of a mile. Indeed, adventurous travellers, who do not mind stooping or even prostration, can make the passage. We preferred to leave it to the more supple and more nimble Arabs, who crouch like cats, and creep and crawl anywhere, under ground or above ground, in the heart of the earth, or up the side of a mountain, and for whom it is a common feat to go in at one entrance and come out at the other. Even while we were at the Pool, a swarthy fellow shot into the darkness, and a few minutes later, as we stood at St. Mary's Well, he reappeared from the bowels of the earth, wet and dripping. This perpetual spring, rising in the very heart of Jerusalem, in the furthest recesses of its rocky bed, and having this double outflow, must have been, when included within the walls, of priceless value to the ancient inhabitants, who in case of siege might otherwise have perished by a water famine. To this the Psalmist refers with pious gratitude when he says, "There is a river the streams whereof make glad the city of God, the holy place of the tabernacles of the Most High."

In making the circuit of the city, another feature comes into view, which it is necessary to understand in order to have a clear idea of the topography of Jerusalem. At the point where the Spring of Siloam issues from the rock, is a ravine descending into the valley, which cuts through the rocky plateau on which the city stands. This is the Tyropœan valley, which, running north and south, cleaves the city in twain, dividing Mount Zion from Mount Moriah, a gorge or chasm once spanned, though at some distance farther up the Tyropœan, by a massive bridge, of which the huge base-stones still remain, over which King Solomon could pass from his palace to the Temple.

And now we sweep round the base of the hill, and leave the Valley of Hinnom to enter the Valley of Jehoshaphat, or of the Kedron—the Black Valley, as the latter name imports, from the rugged and rocky sides which frown over the depth below. The point where the two valleys meet is the lowest depression in the circuit of Jerusalem, being six hundred and seventy feet lower than the highest point on Mount Zion.

As we pass up the Valley of the Kedron, we draw under the shadow (for it is afternoon, and the sun is in the west) of Mount Moriah, and of the walls which enclose the Temple area. Here they rise to their greatest height : for as Moriah descends by a sudden and almost precipitous slope, foundations had to be laid far below in the solid rock, and the superstructure carried far above, to bring this angle of the area on a level with the rest of the plateau on which the Temple stood. Looking upward, a traveller who has come from Britain may be pardoned if he feels a tinge of regret at the absence of a feature which would give at least greater picturesqueness to the fortress-like enclosure—a wish that it were mantled with the ivy which gives such beauty to the castle walls and cathedral towers of England. But it stands bare and naked under the burning Eastern sun. Its very height is masked, and rendered less imposing, by the ruin that has accumulated round its base, which now lies buried under the débris of ages, the wreck of the many sieges in which the ancient walls were thrown down. Explorers have excavated to a depth sufficient to determine that the wall at the southeastern corner was over a hundred and fifty feet high ! This was the pinnacle of the Temple, from which our Lord was tempted to cast himself down. Throned on such a height rose the Temple of Solomon, with its columns of precious stones and its roof of gold. From its position, it could be seen at a great distance. The men of Gad and of Reuben, who dwelt on the other side of the Jordan and of the Dead Sea, as they went up to the top of the mountains of Moab, saw the rising sun reflected back from it; and when the sun went down, the reflection from the other side of the city shone far away over the hills towards the Western Sea. /

But it was not the Temple alone to which the Jew turned with wonder and with pride. In the time of Solomon, when the Hebrew monarchy attained its greatest splendor, Jerusalem was a city of palaces. As Mount Moriah was covered with the Temple, so Mount Zion was covered with palaces, which from its greater height — over a hundred feet above Moriah—were seen at a still greater distance, and must have shown, in the light of the rising or the setting sun, with dazzling splendor.

And now we discover where John found the imagery for the glowing pictures in the Apocalypse of the Mount Zion that is above, the New Jerusalem, that to his enraptured vision seemed to come down from God out of heaven. Those shining walls, that caught the first glimpses of the dawn, and on which lingered the last rays of evening twilight, may well have seemed no unworthy type of the heavenly battlements ; the Gate Beautiful of the gates of pearl ; and the whole majestic Temple to be outshone only by that Celestial City where there is "no temple," and which "has no need of the sun or of the moon to shine in it : for the glory of God doth lighten it, and the Lamb is the light thereof."

As we sauntered along the slopes of the valley, we found that we were walking among the graves of the dead, many of whom, Israelites in race, had lived and perhaps died far from the land of their fathers, but had desired to be buried under the walls of Jerusalem.

From St. Stephen's gate we descended to the brook Kedron, and crossing it, climbed the Mount of Olives, which commands the best view of Jerusalem ; and returning along the northern wall, past the Damascus gate, after an excursion of four hours, reëntered the city by the Jaffa Gate.

Another day we made the circuit of the city on the top of the walls, Dr. Post leading the way with the same elastic step with which he had climbed Mount Serbal. From this point of vantage we looked down into the interior of the city, and saw how it was divided by the Tyropœan Valley, not only into halves but into quarters, by side ravines projecting east and west, so that Jerusalem may be said to stand on four—as Rome stands on seven—hills.

Resting on the tower over the Damascus gate, we looked northward over the more elevated ground on that side of the city which has furnished the only approach for all the besiegers and conquerors of Jerusalem. There spread far and wide the hosts of Nebuchadnezzar, who captured the city and carried away the inhabitants to Babylon. The seventy years of the captivity is one of the sad and melancholy periods of Jewish history, so pathetically and mournfully depicted in the Lamentations of Jeremiah. From this long exile the descendants of those who had been carried away captive, returned to rebuild the walls of Jerusalem. Centuries afterwards the city opened its gates to Alexander the Great. On the same high ground Titus marshalled the Roman legions, and advanced his battering-rams to crush the walls. Later still it became the battle-ground of the Saracens and the Crusaders—of Saladin and Cœur de Lion. So does history pass before us as we stand on the towers of Jerusalem. /

Recalling this long succession of calamities, I wondered not that the Israelites had such downcast and haggard faces. They seemed to carry on their very foreheads all the oppressions and cruelties which have smitten their race. And when I went to the Place of Wailing, and saw men and women, the old and the young, putting their heads against the great foundation-stones of the Temple area, and bemoaning in bitter accents the fate of their city—"O God, the heathen are come into thine inheritance!"—in their cries and tears I seemed to see the woes of all the ages coming upon this generation.

Contempt ceases where pity begins, and pity soon changes to respect. No one can see the bowed heads and weeping eyes, and hear the sobbings which many try in vain to repress, without a great tenderness of feeling for the unhappy Israelites, who after wandering up and down in the earth, have come back to Jerusalem to die.

Nay, the very city itself takes on a new aspect, as it tells in its ruins the history of ages of destruction. I have spoken of the mire of the streets, which is at times almost unfathomable. But there is a history in the very soil beneath our feet, when we recall how it has been fought for by the Maccabees and other brave defenders :

> " Heroes have perished here ;
> 'Tis on their dust ye tread."

Indeed the history of Jerusalem is written in its streets, from the days of Uzziah the King, when it was shaken with an earthquake, which cleft its rocky foundations, and shattered its massive walls. And what battles have raged round these walls! Twenty-seven times has the city been besieged! Babylonian and Assyrian and Egyptian in turn have come up against it, to be followed by Roman and Saracen, Crusader and Turk, who, one and all, have laid waste the holy city, till more than once it has seemed as if there was not left one stone upon another that was not thrown down. Thus Jerusalem has been literally "laid on heaps," till the ancient city has been buried as completely as Pompeii.   As in Rome there is a city under the present city, so there are eight Jerusalems, lying one upon another, like the strata of the rock-ribbed hills.   They are reckoned thus : 1, the city of the Jebusites ; 2, of Solomon ; 3, of Nehemiah ; 4, of Herod, which was destroyed in the siege by Titus in the year 70 ; 5, in the year 130 the Emperor Hadrian began to rebuild it, and it continued under the Roman dominion to the time of the Mohammedan conquest ; 6, the early Moslem ; 7, the city of the Crusaders ; 8, the later Moslem, which still stands ingloriously on the wreck and ruin of all that have preceded it.   In the year 1244 the city was besieged for the last time.   In walking about, we often passed under arches hardly above our heads, which was explained by the fact that the foundations were far down in the earth : arches and walls are buried underground.   Forty feet beneath the Via Dolorosa are Roman pavements, over which passed the victorious legions nearly two thousand years ago. Thus from the very beginning changes have been going on ; from century to century the city has been reconstructed by new creations, and buried again by new destructions, till the dust of Jerusalem is thick with the ashes of a hundred generations.   Reflections like these cause us to lose the feeling of disgust in a melancholy musing and mourning over its decay.   Its very wretchedness becomes—I will not say picturesque : that is too light a word—but mournfully suggestive, as we think of the tale it tells.   " How doth the city sit solitary that was full of people ! how is she become as a widow ! she that was great among the nations ! "   With the crown taken from her head, and no son to restore her fallen greatness, it may be said of her even more than of Rome :

> " The Niobe of nations, there she stands,
>   Crownless and childless in her voiceless woe ! "

As we came back from our excursions day after day, I would trace them out on a map, and try to put in order what we had seen, so as to reconstruct the holy city. Our hotel — the Mediterranean — furnished a good point of observation. As it stood on Mount Zion—think of a hotel on Mount Zion!—it looked down upon Mount Moriah, and into the Temple area, and indeed commanded a view of a large part of the city and of the surrounding country. From the upper story, which was open at one end like a veranda, I could toss a biscuit into the Pool of Hezekiah, which that wise Hebrew king constructed in the heart of the city to supply it with water, as Solomon had constructed the larger Pools which bear his name beyond Bethlehem. A little farther away is a vast enclosure which belongs to the Knights of St. John, and tells of the short century— only eighty-eight years—when the Crusaders were masters of Jerusalem. Turning to the east, one could take in at the same moment the Church of the Holy Sepulchre, where Christian pilgrims were kneeling at their sacred shrines, and the Mosque of Omar, where devout Moslems were bowing, with their faces towards Mecca. Indeed this outlook commands a wider sweep, not only to the Mount of Olives, but far away to the mountains of Moab on the other side of the Dead Sea. /

But we have a nearer object to attract the eye, and touch the imagination. In front of the hotel is an open place, on one side of which stands the Tower of David— one of the oldest and best-preserved monuments in Jerusa-. lem. It is a massive structure, with walls of great strength and height, as if designed to be at once a watch-tower to overlook the city, and a castle for refuge and defence. It is still called the Citadel, and is garrisoned by soldiers. Though built by Herod, it bears the name of the Hebrew King, from an old tradition that David's Palace stood on this very spot. Here was an association to kindle our musings, as we sat on the balcony of our room in the evening, and looked up to the gray old walls. The Passover is always at the time of the full moon, which was now flooding the holy city, and giving a strange, almost ghostly, appearance to its melancholy ruins. As I sat there in the moonlight, there was something in the scene "so sad and fair"—in the clouds that flew across the sky, and the night wind that moaned around the ancient Tower, and died away along the city walls—that set my fancies in motion. Like Bunyan, "I dreamed a dream." Scenes of the past rose before me like visions of the night, and floated away over the Judean hills. Kings and prophets seemed to rise out of their sepulchres ; and of all the Hebrew kings, he who reigned in yonder palace drew most near. Here he gave laws to his people, and perhaps as a warrior gave commands to his armies. From this royal house, it may be, he fled at the conspiracy of Absalom, and here returned, victorious but desolate. Here—perhaps on such a night as this—he looked out of the windows of his palace and sang "The heavens declare the glory of God, and the firmament showeth his handiwork." "When I consider thy heavens, the work of thy fingers, the moon and the stars which thou hast ordained, what is man that thou art mindful of him, and the son of man that thou visitest him?" Here perhaps he breathed his last, and when dying gave to Solomon a charge which might serve for all kings that should ever reign on the earth : "My son, know thou the God of thy father, and serve him with a perfect heart and with a willing mind. . . . If thou seek him, he will be found of thee ; but if thou forsake him, he will cast thee off forever."

Such associations might be multiplied to any extent. If any should question the site of the Palace of David, none will dispute that the Tower was built by Herod, and that if its upper part has been destroyed and rebuilt, at least the massive foundation-stones, to a height of some forty feet, were laid by the King who rebuilt the Temple, and whose pride was in rearing towers and palaces. It was standing when Christ walked these streets : he saw it a thousand times. It is quite probable that he passed it the last night that he spent on earth, on his way to the Cœnaculum, which is farther west on Mount Zion, where he kept the Passover with his disciples. The Paschal moon was shining then, as it is shining now, and perhaps he paused before this Tower to look up to it for the last time. The very next day a Roman soldier standing on its top, and looking down on a scene that was going on just without the city walls, might have been a spectator of the Crucifixion. He would have felt creeping over him a shuddering horror at the mysterious darkening of the earth and sky, and felt the massive foundations under him reeling with the shock of the earthquake, when the rocks were rent and the graves were opened. In the destruction of Jerusalem this Tower was spared by Titus, and stood almost alone amid the mighty ruin ; and so it has remained, sometimes dismantled and broken, yet reconstructed ; and still it stands, and may stand until it sees our Lord coming again in the clouds of Heaven.

With such memories revived by walks about Jerusalem, and meditations in it, how can any one feel that a visit to it in any wise robs it of its charm ? Nay, rather that which was a dream is made a reality ; by familiarizing one's eyes with sacred localities, sacred events are recalled ; the life of our Divine Master becomes more real as we visit the city where he lived and died ; as we pass over the very paths once trodden by his blessed feet ; as we go to the Mount of Olives, where he so often knelt and prayed ; as coming from Bethany, we pause at the spot where, " when he was come near, he beheld the city and wept over it." These are helps, not hindrances, to our faith ; they make the New Testament, in many portions of it, a new book to us. This it is to tread the streets of Jerusalem, until one comes to find pleasure in her stones, because out of these stones he can reconstruct the ancient city, from which came Religion, flowing, like Siloam, out of the heart of the rock, and, like that, making glad the city of God, the holy place of the tabernacles of the Most High. Here we trace to its source much that enters into modern history and modern civilization. A city that has such mighty memories is not dead, but living ; her very woes touch the hearts and the imaginations of men ; and thus she has a power over the world even in her ruins.

# CHAPTER II.

For the greater part of the year Jerusalem is pronounced by most travellers "insufferably dull." Coming
from the life and gayety of European capitals, they are
oppressed by the utter stagnation of a city where there is
no business or commercial life ; where there is not a single
place of amusement, not a theatre, nor even a club ; where
the mail comes but once a week, and there is not even a
newspaper, except a little sheet in Hebrew—a language
with which they are not supposed to be familiar.

But once in the year the sleepy old town awakes from
its long hibernation, as strangers from afar, from beyond
the seas, come riding over the hills, and throng in at the
Jaffa Gate. The Holy Week brings some ten thousand
pilgrims, the greater part of whom find lodging in the
numerous convents, while Englishmen and Americans seek
more comfortable quarters in the hotels. When we were
at the Jordan, at the place of the Baptism, we met an English party, and to our inquiry if there were any strangers
in Jerusalem, a bold Briton answered in language more
emphatic than elegant, that "it was ram-jammed full!"

However, through the kind offices of the American Consul, we found rooms at the Mediterranean Hotel, where we were made very comfortable for the eleven days of our stay.

In the divisions of the "Ecclesiastical Year," of course the first place is given to Holy Week, which is set apart to commemorate the events of our Saviour's last week on earth :—beginning with Palm Sunday, which recalls his entrance into Jerusalem, when the people spread palm branches in the way—including his last supper, betrayal, and crucifixion, his "death and burial "—and ending with Easter, which witnessed his resurrection. This last event is the consummation of our Lord's earthly existence, and of course it is celebrated, with all the events leading up to it, in churches in which there is a great deal of ceremony, with every art to make it impressive. It was to witness this display, in the very cradle of our religion, that we had timed our visit to Jerusalem. ⁄

But if one would see the full pomp of religious cere- monial, he must go to Rome ; or rather, he should have gone in the old days, when the Pope was not " a prisoner," and could appear in the great pageants at the head of his court. It was thirty-four years ago—in 1848, the year of the Revolutions—that I made my first visit to Rome, and spent the Holy Week, and never shall I forget with what pomp it was ushered in. On Palm Sunday the Pope was to bless palms that were to be distributed to the faithful, for which he appeared in state. I was standing in the Piazza of St. Peter's, in a great crowd, when the Supreme Pontiff rode up in a coach with six horses, followed by a body of cavalry. [What a contrast to his Divine Master when he came from Bethany, descending the slope of the Mount of Olives, with no brilliant cortège, but simply riding on an ass—the meek and humble Prince of Peace !]

He was carried into St. Peter's on men's shoulders, and after a while carried out, and then brought in again, and then carried out again! The Cardinals advanced to the foot of the throne, arrayed in costly silks and furs, and knelt to kiss his robe and receive the palms which he blessed ; while the organ pealed, and the Pope's choir, the finest in Europe, was heard through every arch and aisle. At one point, when the voices sank low, and seemed as if wailing over the Saviour's dying agony, the Swiss Guards fell on their knees, bringing down their arms on the pavement so that the vast Cathedral rang again. The effect may be imagined of a scene so grand and mournful, with "the vast and wondrous dome" above, and the kneeling crowds below, hushed in breathless still-ness, while over them swept the wailing voices. Such a scene could not be witnessed anywhere on earth except in Rome—in St. Peter's, the grandest temple ever reared by human hands.

To such pomp as this poor Jerusalem can make no pretension. And yet in one point it has the advantage of Rome, in that "it has not the very images of the things, but the things themselves." One is near, if not upon, the very spot where the events transpired ; and in so far the power of association comes in strongly to aid and stimulate religious devotion./

Desiring to witness at least the beginning of the im-posing services of Holy Week, I was in the Church of the Holy Sepulchre at six o'clock on the morning of Palm Sunday. The Vice-Consul, with his cavass, led the way to the first gallery, from which I could look down on the whole scene. All the Christian communions in Jerusalem were present in gallant array—Latins and Greeks and Ar-menians, Syrians and Copts—bishops and priests bearing palm branches, such as were spread under the Master's

feet as he rode down yonder hill from Bethany on his
entry into Jerusalem. To make a more perfect representation of the original scene, the children sang hosannas. After the palm branches had been duly blessed, they
were passed about in the church and up into the gallery,
not only to the comfort of true believers, but for all who
chose to purchase. An hour or two of this marching
and chanting and incensing, sufficed for me, though the
processions and benedictions were not ended till noon.
But so soon as my curiosity was satisfied, I left the church
for another service, which seemed to me more in harmony
with the spirit of devotion. The Protestant community
in Jerusalem is a very small one, yet to-day there were
strangers from all parts of the earth, among whom were
many of our own faith and language, with whom it was
delightful to walk to the house of God in company. The
English church on Mount Zion was filled, as it is only in
the Holy Week, by a congregation that included representatives even from the antipodes. A bishop from New
Zealand preached from the text "And when he was come
near, he beheld the city, and wept over it." In the front
pew, under the pulpit, sat the young English princes, who,
having made the circuit of the globe, had returned by way
of the Red Sea, and after a short stay in Egypt, had come
to Jerusalem. The elder, the heir to the throne, who
in his name, Albert Victor, unites the names of both
grandfather and grandmother, is tall and slender, with
very much the figure that his father had when he visited
America in 1860. It was pleasant to see him joining in
the singing, and responding reverently in the service,
and thus conforming, at least in outward respect, to the
worship of the Church of England, of which he is to be
the royal head. The younger, Prince George of Wales,
was looking about, as if he were more interested in the

congregation than in the service. He is a mere boy, but is a great favorite with his shipmates for his brightness and gayety. When the service was ended, the princes went out first. They were very simply dressed, with small, slouched hats, and pantaloons turned up to keep them out of the mud. So far as one could judge from merely seeing them in public, they seemed to be good specimens of Young England, and certainly produced a favorable impression on others than their own countrymen by their absence of pretension and unaffected simplicity. /

With Monday we were rested, and in a mood for seeing the sights of Jerusalem, or attending the services of Holy Week. Our first visit was to the Armenian Convent. The principal buildings of the modern Jerusalem are those erected by different Christian communions for their brethren in the holy city. If there are no princes in Jerusalem, the patriarchs may be considered as princes, and the convents are their palaces. The Armenian Convent covers many acres of ground, like one of the great ecclesiastical houses of Europe ; and includes within its ample walls not only the Convent proper, or Monastery, but the residence of the patriarch, and of the attending priests, who form around him a kind of ecclesiastical court, and also places for the reception and entertainment of the annual pilgrims. Dr. Post wished to take me to the Convent to introduce me to the Patriarch, of whom he spoke as not only an acquaintance, but a personal friend, which I could well believe when I saw the way in which they fell into each other's arms and embraced in true Oriental style. The Patriarch lives in a good deal of state, as becomes one whose authority extends over one of the largest Christian bodies in the East. As he did not speak English nor French, nor even Arabic, but only Turkish and Armenian, we had to converse with him through an interpreter. But no barrier of language could intercept the warmth of his welcome. He was extremely courteous, and offered us the hospitality of his Convent, wishing us to be his guests for weeks. It was almost embarrassing to receive this pressing invitation from one whose graciousness of manner was heightened by a charming presence, which made it hardly possible to refuse him. I felt that he was made to be an ecclesiastical dignitary. His form was portly ; his face benignant ; nor could there be a finer figure-head to appear in great ecclesiastical ceremonies, or to lead the processions in the Church of the Holy Sepulchre. I cannot say that

"On his brow deliberation sat,
    And public care " : /

for indeed he seemed to have an easy time of it, while he was receiving the homage of the faithful, and bestowing his benediction. As we rose to take leave, he accompanied us into the church, and had its treasures, including his own jewels and costly vestments, brought out for our inspection ; and when we took our departure, he sprinkled us, according to an Oriental custom, with rose-water. Hardly had we returned to our hotel before a monk followed us, bearing a tray loaded with sweetmeats ! What a dainty thing it is to be a Patriarch, scattering smiles, distributing bon-bons, and sprinkling rose-water ! But I would not give the impression that he has no higher ideas of his holy office. His courtesy does not prevent his being a zealous bishop of his large flock. It is said that he preaches to the pilgrims of his creed, who come to Jerusalem (sometimes two or three thousand take up their quarters in the Convent) with great plainness and fidelity. Thus his character commands respect, while his welcome was of the sort that leaves a grateful feeling behind it. He seemed to wish to keep me in memory, by requesting my photograph, which of course I blushingly declined.

Dr. Post, however, appropriated it, and sent it to him; and he returned the compliment by sending me his own handsome face, with his autograph, and a rosary which he had blessed, and which I keep, not for any mysterious virtue that it possesses, but as a memento of an accomplished dignitary of his Church.

Jerusalem is a city of many races and many religions. If the degree of devotion is to be judged by the multiplicity of faiths and forms of worship, it must take high rank among cities, because of the religions which it embraces in such number and variety. Here one may find the Jew in his synagogue, and the Moslem in his mosque; while the Christian community is divided between Latins and Greeks, Armenians, Syrians, and Copts, the increase to the population from travellers only adding to the confusion, as it is made up of representatives of all the sects of Europe and America./

Yet though the forms of religion be so many, Judaism is the mother of them all, and it is largely represented in its ancient capital. One quarter of the city is set apart for the Jews, who come here from all parts of the world, and form a community by themselves. Generally they are poor, and are supported by the liberality of their richer brethren in Europe. They crowd together in the narrow streets on Mount Zion, and may easily be distinguished, not only by their peculiar physiognomies, but by their long gabardines and fur caps, from under which corkscrew curls, falling down their cheeks, give their faces a feminine and affected appearance. But one cannot look without respect on the representatives of an ancient race and ancient worship. I was in a reverential mood when I was presented to the Chief Rabbi, a venerable old gentleman, though not wearing the majestic air, any more than the sweeping robes, of the High Priest of the ancient Temple. We visited a number of the synagogues, some of which are very ancient. One or two of them may have been standing—or their predecessors on the same sites—in the time of our Saviour. It was not the hour of service, and but a few Israelites were present, who were sitting about tables reading out of the books of the law, or of Ezra or Nehemiah, or other prophets. Such is their reverence for the law that they have the Ten Commandments engraved on silver, and bind it as a frontlet on their foreheads, or on a silver scroll and embedded in the door-posts, which they kiss as they pass, as a devout Catholic dips his fingers in holy water. But I did not observe in the synagogues the silent prayer and appearance of deep devotion which one so often sees in Catholic churches and cathedrals.

Still more interesting was it to witness the celebration of the Passover, for which we were taken to one of the chief hospitals in Jerusalem. Of course the Hebrews whom we saw here were not of the highest social position ; they were all poor, or aged, or infirm, of a condition which made them fit inmates of an hospital. But their poverty did not abate their national pride or religious zeal, or the fervor with which they entered into the ceremony. One who has anything of the historical spirit cannot fail to be interested in a festival which dates back, not like our Thanksgiving, to the landing of the Pilgrims less than three centuries ago, but to an event more than thirty centuries old—to that fatal night when the angel of the Lord passed through the land of Egypt and smote the first-born, and the Israelites, who sprinkled blood on the door-posts of their houses, were passed by.

The attendants were grouped about a long table, at which they read the account of the original Passover, and passages from the Psalms and the Prophets. I observed that they did not read in Hebrew, but in Spanish, and learned that a large part of the Jews in Jerusalem are from Spain, who with the Jews from Germany and Poland, make up the great body of their race who are here. The Spanish Jews are of a superior class to the wretched wanderers from the North of Europe, who have found their way back to Jerusalem to die. Their reading was relieved at intervals by partaking of a repast set before them, which, though it was of a rude simplicity, (unleavened bread and a platter of bitter herbs,) as if prepared in haste for an army in flight, was ample in quantity, and of which they partook with hearty appetites, especially as this frugal fare was made palatable by abundant potations, with which it is a custom,

" More honored in the breach than the observance,"

to refresh themselves very freely. A Catholic priest once quoted to me with relish the saying of a devout Irishman, who wished to express his gratitude for the mode of observance of one of the appointed fasts of the Church : "Blessin's on the Council o' Trint, that it put the fastin' on the mate, an' not on the dhrink ! " These pious Hebrews seemed to be of the same mind, so that I was not much surprised to be told that the feast not seldom ended—as what are profanely called Christian feasts and festivals sometimes end—by leaving the celebrants helpless on the floor !

But one does not feel like bringing an accusation against a people that are so poor and wretched. In visiting their hospitals and their schools, I was glad to see that they were not forgotten by the rich Hebrew bankers and other wealthy Jews in the capitals of Europe. The Rothschilds and Sir Moses Montefiore especially, have distinguished themselves by their generous liberality towards their brethren. One must rejoice in anything thus done for a people and a city which are dear alike to every Jewish and every Christian heart throughout the world.

The Moslem worship is more imposing than the Jewish. I can never hear unmoved the cry of the muezzin from the minaret which calls the faithful to prayer, or see the robed figures turned towards Mecca, and bowed to the earth. The Moslems are masters of Jerusalem, and of all the sacred sites of the Holy City. Even the place where stood the Temple of Solomon, is now occupied by the Mosque of Omar. It is but a few years since all access was sternly forbidden ; no Christian could enter except at the risk of his life. When Dean Stanley first visited Jerusalem, he could see into the Temple area only from the Mount of Olives, or from some other high point which looked down upon it. But even though he had to sketch from a distance, yet never was the picture more perfectly drawn than by the hand of this consummate artist. Speaking of the Mosque of Omar, and the effect of grandeur it gives to Jerusalem, he says : /

"From whatever point that graceful dome, with its beautiful precinct, emerges to view, it at once dignifies the whole city. And when from Olivet, or from the Governor's house, or from the north-east wall, you see the platform on which it stands, it is a scene hardly to be surpassed. A dome graceful as that of St. Peter's, though of course on a far smaller scale, rising from an elabo-rately-finished circular edifice; this edifice raised on a square marble platform, rising on the highest ridge of a green slope, which descends from it north, south, and east, to the walls sur-rounding the whole enclosure ; platform and enclosure diversified by lesser domes and fountains, by cypresses and olives and planes and palms ; the whole as secluded and quiet as the interior of some college or cathedral garden, only enlivened by the white figures of veiled women stealing like ghosts up and down the green slope, or by the turbaned heads bowed low in the various niches for prayer. This is the Mosque of Omar; the Haram es-Sherif, 'the noble sanctuary'; the second most sacred spot in the Mahometan world—that is, the next after Mecca ; the second most beautiful mosque—that is, the next after Cordova."/

This picture so beautiful he could only see at a distance ;

this enclosure he was not permitted to enter. But he partly
consoles himself for it by saying :

"I for one felt almost disposed to console myself for the exclu-
sion by the additional interest which the sight derives from the
knowledge that no European foot, except by stealth or favor, had
ever trodden within these precincts since the Crusaders were driven
out, and that their deep seclusion was as real as it appeared. It
needed no sight of the daggers of the black dervishes, who stand
at the gate, to tell you that the Mosque was undisturbed and inviolably sacred."/

But now the daggers of the black dervishes are
sheathed, and though there may be scowling faces and
muttered curses, still the gates which for six centuries
were shut in the face of the whole Christian world, are
thrown open, and we may enter the precincts which till
recently were "inviolably sacred." We did not have to
disguise ourselves in Oriental costume, but wore our
customary Frank dress, and walked in openly, "no man
forbidding us"; and when we came to the Mosque itself,
not only were the doors open, but the old custodian, with
backsheesh in his eye, received us with a suppleness
and graciousness that were truly Oriental. Here is that
famous rock, covered by the dome of the Mosque of
Omar, which has so puzzled antiquarians—whether it be
the rock on which Abraham bound Isaac for the sacrifice,
or the threshing-floor of Ornan the Jebusite, where the
plague was stayed. Fortunately the identity of the
Temple area has never been doubted. True, there is a
question as to the exact spot in it on which stood the
Temple of Solomon, some placing it on the very site of the
Mosque of Omar, others on that of the Mosque of Aksa in
one corner of the large enclosure. There is also a question whether any part of the substructure remains from
the time of Solomon. Sir Charles Wilson, who made the
Ordnance Survey, the results of which have been pub-

lished by the English Government in several large volumes, is now in Jerusalem, and tells me that he can find nothing earlier than the time of Herod. Captain Warren, however, gives an earlier date to the lower courses of Cyclopean masonry in the eastern wall, and to the huge foundation-stones at Robinson's Arch and the Place of Wailing, which he assigns to the time of Solomon. But even if they were of the architecture of Herod, they were standing in the time of Christ, so that the Temple area was substantially then as now. All this ground was familiar to the eyes and to the feet of our Lord. Here he stood and cried (perhaps seeing the libations of water brought in a golden vessel from Siloam), "If any man thirst, let him come unto me and drink." Here was one of the strong positions in the defence of Jerusalem, into which burst the army of Titus on the fearful night that the city was taken, when a soldier, in violation of the express order of his commander, threw a torch into the Temple; and suddenly the captured city and the encircling hills, and the sky itself, were illumined by the mighty conflagration. In that flame and smoke went down the hope of Israel for centuries, and perhaps for millenniums.

But the great interest of Jerusalem during the Holy Week, is neither Jewish nor Moslem, but Christian. While we have been making the circuit of the walls, or visiting mosques or synagogues, the crowd of pilgrims within the gates has been, day after day, surging towards one sacred spot—the Church of the Holy Sepulchre, within which are witnessed the grand ceremonies at this season of the Christian year. But this is a subject by itself.

# CHAPTER III.

## THE CHURCH OF THE HOLY SEPULCHRE—FEET-WASHING BY THE GREEK PATRIARCH.

Standing on the top of the Tower of David, and looking down upon Jerusalem, one sees lying almost in the heart of the city an ancient architectural pile, whose dome covers the holiest shrine in the Christian world. This is the Church of the Holy Sepulchre, which includes within its walls both the rock of Calvary, on which our Lord was crucified, and the tomb in which his body was laid, and from which he rose on the third day. I am well aware of the disputes as to the identity of these sites. Certainly this could *not* have been the place of the Crucifixion, if it was always, as now, in the heart of the city : for Jesus went forth bearing his cross, and suffered without the gate. And yet, in spite of all objections, Col. Wilson, the American Consul, who has been here for several years, and made a study of the question, is very positive in his conviction that the sites are genuine, and that Calvary and the Sepulchre are both properly included in the same enclosure. Many others, whose opinions are at least worthy of respect, agree with him. Further than stating what *they* think, I have no disposition to go : for however the balance of probabilities may seem to incline one way or the other, it must be very unsatisfactory to discuss a question which cannot be definitely settled till farther explorations have determined the exact position of the second wall of Jerusalem.

Perhaps the incredulity would not be so great if the difficulties were not multiplied by the multiplication of sites : for not only is the place of Calvary fixed here, and of the Sepulchre, but all of the minor sites that can be in any way connected with these, each of which is identified with the utmost precision : such as the very spot where our Lord was mocked ; where he was scourged, with a fragment of the column to which he was bound ; where he was nailed to the cross ; where the soldiers cast lots for his raiment, and the women anointed his body ; the stone which was rolled from the door of the Sepulchre, and on which the angel sat ; and the spot where Christ appeared to Mary Magdalene. Thus at every step one finds some new site, till the Church becomes a kind of sacred museum, in which objects the most diverse are gathered together. It seems highly improbable that even its broad roof could cover so many spots of sacred interest. The number is too great to be included even within its ample walls. It could hardly be explained except on the theory of miraculous interposition, that all these sites should be grouped in one circumference ; and the attempt to bring them together throws an air of suspicion over the whole, as if it were all a monkish fable and superstition. /

Some are so shocked and disgusted at the fables that are told of these " holy places," that they cannot visit with pleasure any spot which tradition has invested with sacredness, because of the superstitious fancies and follies with which it is sure to be connected. Even my dear Dr. Post feels this so strongly that he turns away from holy shrines with an instinct of aversion, as from impostures which in many cases are so gross that no pains are taken at concealment.

But for my part, I am not careful to answer in these things, for if that which is assumed be *not* established—even if the identity be more than doubtful—still there is an association which of itself gives interest to the spot, and a great power over the imagination. A church which the tradition of the whole Christian world for sixteen hundred years has accepted as the place of burial of our Lord—for the possession of which great wars have been waged—is at least a historical monument of the deepest interest. The Crusades were undertaken to recover the Holy Sepulchre, which was believed to be within the walls of this church. A sanctuary to recover which Europe and the East were at war for a century, must be regarded as one of the historical buildings of the world, and cannot be approached without a feeling of veneration.

But more than that, it has not only historical interest, but religious interest. Whether it be the spot of our Lord's entombment, or no, yet the very belief invests it with a tender interest. The association makes it sacred ; it has been consecrated by the faith and hope, by the tears and prayers, of generations. As such I enter it with a feeling of reverence, if not of devotion, and stand with uncovered head amid the throng of kneeling worshippers. /

Although the Holy Week begins with Palm Sunday, the more impressive services do not commence till Thursday, the anniversary of that last Passover which our Lord kept with his disciples the evening before his death. His betrayal by Judas on that night was the beginning of his "Passion," which gives Holy Week the name of Passion Week. From this moment the interest deepens as the scene darkens. The darkness deepens till the Lord of

glory expires, when it is the midnight of the world ; and
this darkness hangs like a pall over the earth till the
morning of the third day, when as the sun rises in the
East, the Son of Man rises from the tomb.  Thus within
three days the mind passes — as did the minds of the
disciples when waiting in fearful suspense — from  the
depths of despair to the height of joy.

Thursday morning I had gone to the American Consul's
to listen to the chain of proofs which he had kindly offered
to give me, for the faith that is in him in regard to the
identity of the principal sites in the Church of the Holy
Sepulchre.  He is a full believer, and supports his position
with an array of learning which I was quite unable, even
if I had been disposed, to answer.  [He afterwards went
with me to the Church itself, and to the Porta Judiciaria,
on the Via Dolorosa, to point out local indications which
satisfied him of the truth of his position.]/

While listening to this most interesting explanation,
Dr. Post came in haste to bid me come instantly to see the
crowd gathering to witness the Washing of Feet by the
Greek Patriarch.  This is one of the sights of Holy Week
in Jerusalem that must not be omitted.  We hastened
across the street, and down the steps into the court, where
we found a great concourse in a state of excitement, in
which there was apparently more of curiosity than of devotion.  Not only was the open space packed with a dense
mass of human beings, but the roofs of the adjoining buildings were covered ; every window was full of eager faces ;
indeed swarthy fellows, with strong hands and nimble feet,
were climbing to every capstone or projecting bit of wall
on which a monkey could sit, to look down on the strange
scene.  In the centre of the open square was a raised platform occupied by a dozen priests or pilgrims, who were
waiting, not apparently in a mood of devotion, but in that

flutter of excitement which may be seen round the galleries at Yale or Harvard on Commencement Day. It was a grand spectacle, in which they were actors, and they enjoyed for their little hour being made conspicuous. After long waiting a stir in the crowd announced the approach of the Greek Patriarch, who, with all the pomp and dignity of Eastern ceremonial, in vestments covered with gold and fairly weighted with jewels, was ushered to his seat, where he appeared as our Lord, while "the twelve" who sat round him personated the Apostles. In this sacred drama each one had his separate part. It was easy to distinguish John, the beloved disciple, as he leaned on the bosom of his Lord. All these tender scenes, best imagined in the shades of evening, in the still upper room, were dragged into the garish light of day, to be made a spectacle to the gaping multitude. When it came to the feet-washing, the Patriarch, laying aside his costly vestments, girded himself with a towel, in imitation of his Divine Master, and began to wash the feet of those who represented the Apostles—and not only washed them, but kissed them! When he came to Peter, that ardent and impulsive, but somewhat refractory, Apostle went into frantic demonstrations, as if he would forbid such an act of humiliation on the part of his Lord—a resistance which was at last overcome, and he yielded with well-feigned reluctance. /

When all was over, the Patriarch retired to his Convent to rest after his fatigues. An hour or two later we called by appointment for an interview, and were told that "His Beatitude" was taking his repose. However, he soon awoke from his slumbers, and appeared in his grand salon, smiling and gracious. Of course all well-bred travellers treat him with the respect due to his high office ; but I could not quite repress a secret thought that it was a little out of character for one who had taken the chief part in

such sacred scenes, to be making pleasant speeches to the
ladies, and clinking glasses with the gentlemen!

After the interview, we walked in the garden, among
the orange trees, and thought what "a sweet thing" it was
to be a Patriarch, with no children to look after, unless he
regards as such the members of his spiritual household.
And if any of them appear unruly, they are easily disposed
of : for not far away is the Convent of Mar Saba, to which
a turbulent ecclesiatic can be "advised" to retire for
meditation and prayer ; and if a longer withdrawal from
the world be thought for his spiritual benefit, he may be
counselled to follow the example of Paul, and spend three
years in Arabia, among the cliffs of Sinai.  I could not forget our old friend, the Archimandrite of Jerusalem, at the
Convent of St. Catherine, who, I doubt not, is there yet,
and will remain so long as "His Beatitude" may think
best to keep him there.  The sleek Patriarch is a perfect
autocrat in his spiritual dominion, and can banish at his
will any wretched priest or monk who may incur his dis-
pleasure.  It seemed uncharitable to think that this smiling old man might conceal under his soft raiment a heart
as hard and cruel as ever sent a heretic to the prison of
the Inquisition.  I say not that it is so ; he may be a very
kind-hearted man.  But there is nothing in his position to
prevent his playing the tyrant as fully as any Turkish
pasha.  Here is the danger of ecclesiastical power : it is
the paw of the lion, soft to the touch, but with a terrible
gripe to crush and to destroy.

What a contrast to this scene was the communion at
the English church, which is always celebrated on Thursday evening of Holy Week—"the same night in which he
was betrayed."  It was a help to our thoughts that we had
just paid a visit to the Cœnaculum, which is on Mount
Zion, and not far away, the chamber in which, according

to tradition, our Lord kept his last Passover with his disciples. It may indeed be on the site, but certainly this pillared hall is not the "upper room" : for it is in a style of architecture unknown in the time of our Saviour. The arches which support the ceiling are not Roman, but Gothic, giving the room the appearance of a monks' refectory in an old English abbey. This indicates that it is of a date not earlier than the time of the Crusaders. Still a visit which recalled the event could not but deepen the impression of the service that was to follow. Listening to the reading of the account of the original institution, we seemed to hear the Master's voice saying "Do this in remembrance of me." After an earnest discourse by another Australian bishop, the communion was celebrated ; and it was a touching thought that we were partaking of the Last Supper in Jerusalem on the very night on which our Lord was betrayed, and not far from the spot where he sat down with the twelve.

After the service in the church, Dean Howson of Chester (so well known in America by the admirable work, Conybeare and Howson's Life and Travels of St. Paul) and a few others went out to the Mount of Olives, and there—a little above the enclosed Garden of Gethsemane, and nearer, as they thought, to the exact spot, under some ancient olives—read the story of Christ's agony in the Garden, and knelt and prayed where he had prayed before them. It was a moment long to be remembered. Who that has once heard can ever forget how Antoinette Sterling used to sing

> " 'Tis midnight, and on Olive's brow
> The star is dimmed that lately shone ;
> 'Tis midnight, and on Olive's brow
> The suffering Saviour prays alone " ?

Such memories now returned with the place and the

hour. It was a strange, weird scene, the lights shining through the trees, recalling that night when Judas and the band of soldiers came "with lanterns" along this same slope. Just as they closed their service, the full moon— the Paschal moon—rose above the crest of Olivet, and shone down into the Valley of the Kedron, and on the gray old walls of the city beyond. /

Good Friday is celebrated in a manner peculiarly Oriental. It is natural that the hearts of devout pilgrims should be stirred at finding themselves on the very day of the Crucifixion on the spot where it took place, and that they should desire to recall in some impressive form a scene so grand and awful. But the method taken is more fitted to dispel than to deepen the impression of solemnity. It is a kind of "Passion Play," which is so forced and unnatural that it has not at all the pathos of that at Ober-Ammergau, where the mournful scenes are depicted by simple and devout peasants amid the sombre surroundings of the Bavarian Alps. There it is a man who personates the Christ, and who is lifted on the cross in an attitude which shows extreme bodily tension and suffering, from which he is often taken down in a swoon. But here there is no quivering flesh and blood, but only a wooden figure, which is mocked and scourged, and into which are driven the nails, and which is then lifted upon the cross, and after- wards taken down and borne to the "Stone of Unction" to be anointed for burial, and placed in the sepulchre. The effect may be imagined in a church filled with a dense crowd, whose upturned faces are eager and excited. At each pause in the tragic scene a brief sermon is delivered, so that in the whole there are half a dozen in as many different languages. Such a mingling of the theatrical with the religious is well fitted to rouse the superstition and fanaticism of the spectators, but not to leave a lasting impression of the awful event which it is intended to commemorate. ⸌

While these demonstrations were more painful than solemn, there was one silent recognition of the day that was very impressive—the flags were hung at half mast! This I had never seen before in any of the cities of Christendom, and that drooping symbol told the story of death as no words could tell it. It was as if the Lord had just expired on the cross ; as if his body had just been laid in the sepulchre, and the disciples were looking into one another's faces in speechless sorrow — a spectacle which might well touch the hearts of all beholders, not only with sympathy but with awe ; as in the original scene, " the people that came together to that sight, beholding the things that were done, smote their breasts and returned." The commemoration of such events awakens a feeling which seeks relief in worship and in prayer. Again the English Church presented a welcome place of retreat, where Dean Howson preached an excellent sermon from the text " The inscription was written in Hebrew, in Greek, and in Latin," from which he drew a lesson most fitting to the day, that the very words above our Saviour's drooping head, though undesigned by the Roman soldiers who placed them there, being in different languages, indicated that the offering which he then made was not for one nation only, but for men of all tongues and climes, for all the tribes and kindreds of mankind. ⁄

# CHAPTER IV.

## THE GREEK FIRE, SUPPOSED TO BE LIGHTED BY THE DESCENT OF THE HOLY GHOST.

/The great day of the Holy Week in Jerusalem is not, as in Rome, Good Friday, the Day of the Crucifixion ; nor Easter, the Day of the Resurrection ; but the day between, Saturday. Then the scene of suffering is over : the long agony has ended in death. No more can the disciples gather round their beloved Master ; no more can they hear his voice, saying "Let not your hearts be troubled ; ye believe in God, believe also in me." He is gone to the grave. It is the hour and the power of darkness. At this moment, when darkness covers the earth, fire from heaven descends to reillumine the light that has been extinguished. As of old the Holy Ghost descended in tongues of fire on the heads of the Apostles, so now does a heavenly flame flash from above to kindle the torches of the faithful who are waiting to receive it, and to cast light again upon a darkened world. |

Such is the theory, and such the ceremony witnessed every year in the Church of the Holy Sepulchre. So gross is the imposture that long since the Latins refused to have anything to do with it ; and the Greeks, while they continue the observance, are forced to disclaim its miraculous pretensions. When the Patriarch received us with such benignity, an inquisitive American might have felt tempted to seek enlightenment on this point, but we could not so far disturb his calmness as to ask such troublesome questions. But the priest who officiated as his interpreter, said to us privately that His Beatitude did not claim for it a miraculous, but only a symbolic character. Yet he knew very well that whatever explanations he might give to travellers, the people *did* believe in the holy fire in its most literal interpretation ; that it came from heaven ; and that this, and this alone, led them to regard it with such awe. The Patriarch may wash his hands, like Pilate, and protest that he is innocent, but he lends his name and presence to one of the most shameless superstitions of modern times.

How great is the credulity of the people is shown by the fact that they regard it as an object of envy and ambition to be the *first* to catch the sacred flame, and are willing to pay for the privilege. It is put up at auction, being cried aloud in the church by a priest, who asks "Who will part with earthly goods to obtain a heavenly inheritance?" On this occasion a wealthy Armenian was the highest bidder, paying sixty pounds for the first place! Is it to be supposed that one of this thrifty race, which has the reputation of always looking out for the main chance, would throw away such a sum for a torch lit by a lucifer match? No ; he believed that it was lighted by the same Holy Ghost who descended in tongues of fire on the Apostles. The fame of this keen rivalry for the heavenly prize went abroad in Jerusalem, and added to the eagerness to be present. Dr. Post had left that day for Jaffa, to take the steamer for Beirut, being obliged to return to his family and his College ; so that I was alone, and should not have dared to venture into such a crowd, but by the kindness of the Consul, I was accompanied on this, as on other occasions, by a potent protector, in the person of the cavass. Whoever has been in the East has had frequent occasion to exclaim, Great is the cavass! This is the attendant of an official—a sort of body-guard, who goes before him and clears the way, and who in outward appearance is a much more imposing figure than his master. He was got up in grand costume, with baggy trousers and braided coat, and carried in his hand a huge truncheon loaded at the bottom, which rang as he struck it on the pavement, a sign that somebody was coming ; and a warning to "everybody," that was not "somebody," to get out of the way. This cavass was a *striking* character in more ways than one, for he did not hesitate to give, if not a blow, at least a vigorous push, to any one who did not move fast enough. The crowd, packed as it was, opened right and left, thinking no doubt that it was some grand personage, a Governor or a Pasha, who was walking with majestic presence behind. If they had only known that it was only a private American citizen ! Not for the world would I let them into the secret, but walked with head erect and unmoved countenance, as if I were a sovereign, (as I am : are not all Americans sovereigns?) and their marks of reverence were but the just and proper recognition of my personal consequence ! /

And so, following this majestic creature, he led me through the court and into the church, where the soldiers kept a passage clear. We stepped quickly through till we reached the foot of a stair which led up into a gallery. There are several galleries, one above the other, which, as they afford commanding positions, are kept for invited guests, or for travellers who pay for reserved seats. Above us stood a group of dignitaries of the Church of England, among whom shone the face of good Dean Howson. I was in what would be called in a theatre "the first tier," just opposite the Chapel of the Holy Sepulchre, where I had paid half a napoleon (two dollars) for a front seat, from which I looked down on the whole scene.

And what a scene it was! To say that the church was full, conveys no idea of the compact mass that was wedged into it. I find it difficult to estimate the capacity of a building which is neither square nor round, nor confined within four walls, but runs off into side chapels and passages. It is said that altogether it will hold over six thousand. As this was the great spectacle of the week, of course the pilgrims—at least the Greek pilgrims—were anxious to see it. Hundreds had slept in the church all night to keep their places for the next day. In the rear of the galleries were heaps of blankets, on which they had snatched a brief repose. And when to this was added the entrance from without, the crush was tremendous. The Turkish soldiers tried to keep back the incoming multitude, but in vain. Such was the fever of excitement that it could not be restrained. In it rolled like a tide, surging in every direction, with a noise like the roaring of the sea. /

The tumult and the uproar could only be compared to that at some mass meeting or political convention. Instead of the great assembly being hushed in awe, the body of those on the pavement of the church were singing as in chorus. "What mean these wild voices?" I asked of one of the attachés of the Consulate who stood beside me. "It is the Greeks," he answered. "And what are they saying?" (for I heard the same words oft repeated.) "They are singing 'This is the tomb of our Lord who redeemed us by his blood!'" So far well, and if the voices were loud and piercing, still they might be taken as the irrepressible outcry of faith, as when the multitude shouted

Hosannas. But hark what follows : "We are happy, *but the Jews are miserable!* " The jubilant strains of the Greeks were mingled with that hatred of another race and another religion which is a part of their "orthodox faith " ; at the very moment of their exultation at being redeemed by the Saviour's blood, their mouths were filled with cursing and bitterness. It seemed that they could not express their own religious joy without intermingling with it their hatred of others. It was said that if a Jew had dared to show his head within the church at that moment, he would have been torn in pieces, unless he had been rescued by the Turkish soldiers.

Looking down upon this mass swaying to and fro, I was in terror lest some of the weaker ones in the crowd, unable to keep their standing, should be thrown down and trampled under foot. It is not an infrequent occurrence that persons suffer great bodily injuries, and that some are even crushed to death. The chief struggle was around the Chapel of the Sepulchre, which was to be the scene of the supernatural display. The Chapel has on its side a large round opening, like a port-hole, through which would be thrust the flaming torch that was lighted from heaven ; and the great object was to be near this holy aperture, so as to be the first to snatch the sacred fire. Foremost of those who pushed towards this spot were a number of young men, with bared arms and legs, stripped as for a race. As they came forward, the soldiers tried to push them back, and I was fearful that to the scene of crushing would now be added the more horrible spectacle of fighting in this holy place. It is not uncommon for the soldiers and the pilgrims to come to blows. Indeed on one memorable occasion, in 1834, there was a conflict, in which three hundred were killed, and the pavement ran with blood. But the men stood their ground, and for a few

moments kept up an altercation with the officers, in which
I surmised that they were explaining that they were either
representatives of the rich Armenian who had bought the
first place, or men who had themselves paid for the next
places, and so had a right to be there—points which the
Turks at last got into their dull heads, and yielded a little,
and allowed the persistent devotees to come up closer till
they could hug the very walls ; and here they stood, cling-
ing to the marble till the fire from heaven should descend.

At length order was in some degree restored, and the
crowd pushed back by the soldiers, so as to open a circular
space round the Chapel of the Sepulchre, and then entered
a series of processions. First came the Greek Patriarch,
followed by his clergy in their most gorgeous robes, carrying banners and chanting the litanies. Thus moving
with slow step to the sound of their solemn music, they
circled three times round the Holy Sepulchre. Next came
the Armenians, whose Patriarch outshone his Greek brother in the splendor of his episcopal costume ; and then
the other Oriental sects—the Copts, the Syrians, and the
Abyssinians.

The processions ended, there came the supreme moment, when the Greek Patriarch entered the Holy Sepulchre. All lights were extinguished, and the church was in
darkness. Then for the first time there was silence. The
whole vast assembly stood breathless, while the Patriarch,
having like the High Priest entered into the Holy of
Holies, was bowed in prayer. It was a moment of eager
expectation. In this deep stillness, out of the darkness
suddenly the light appeared. From where I stood, I saw
the first faint glimmer within the recess. Long arms had
been stretched within the aperture to grasp it, and in an
instant it flashed in the eyes of the great assembly, those
who seized it first holding it aloft in triumph. Then fol-

lowed a scene which defies description. A hundred arms were outstretched to catch the fire, and in an instant it flew from hand to hand, till in a space of time so brief that it seemed almost instantaneous, the whole building was aflame. From below the torches were passed up into the galleries, and were flashed in our faces. The ladies shrunk back lest their dresses should be caught. We all seemed to be in danger. Perhaps we were to be offered up as sacrifices on an altar. As Nero bound the Christians to columns, and smeared them with pitch, and set them on fire to light the Imperial gardens, so we might in the same way obtain the honors of martyrdom ; or we might perish, not alone, but with the venerable church itself as a funeral pile : for indeed for a few moments I felt a degree of alarm lest the ancient shrine should take fire, as gallery above gallery was in a blaze, while the dome was filled with smoke as with a cloud of incense.

Nor was the illumination confined within the walls. Torches were passed without to the vast crowd waiting in the court. The men whom we had seen round the Holy Sepulchre stripped for the race, were torch-bearers, and now bounded away through the city streets, and out of the gates, speeding over hill and valley to carry the sacred flame to distant hamlets and homes scattered among the hills and valleys of Judea. These torches are precious heirlooms to the pilgrims. After being lighted for a time, they are extinguished, but kept with religious care, to be relighted again only at a bridal or a burial. When the time comes that a service for the dead is to be prepared, they are placed like candles upon the altar, so that those who, having once made the pilgrimage to Jerusalem, now make a longer pilgrimage, may be said to be lighted to the grave by torches first kindled by fire from heaven.

The spectacle was over. We had been in the church

nearly four hours, but it was a long time before the crowd dispersed, so excited were they by this miraculous descent of the Holy Ghost. As I walked slowly away, I was in a sad mood at such a representation of Christianity in the cradle of our religion. Was there ever a more melancholy exhibition of human folly, and folly associated with some of the worst passions of our nature? Fanaticism and superstition go together. One form of madness leads to another, and religious enthusiasm, uncontrolled, lends itself to hatred, malice, and all uncharitableness. It is the same thing the world over, in all ages and all countries. The crowd that filled the theatre at Ephesus, and shouted " Great is Diana of the Ephesians ! " was not a whit more frenzied with the fanaticism of superstition, than the Greeks whom I saw in the evening (when I came again before the church was filled, and when there was space to move about), actually *running* round the Holy Sepulchre like demons, shouting " O Jews ! Jews ! your feast is a feast of devils or of murderers, but our feast is the feast of Christ ! "/

As it happened, that same afternoon I went to the Temple area, and the change was very great from the scene I had witnessed to the quiet of this peaceful spot. As we entered the gate, the muezzin was calling the faithful to prayer. All was still, as became a place of worship. In the seclusion of the sheltered enclosure, and the reverent manner of those whose heads were bowed in prayer, there was something far more in harmony with the spirit of devotion than what we had just seen, and I could not but think that for religious worship the Mosque of Omar presented a favorable contrast with the Church of the Holy Sepulchre.

The next morning was Easter, and the day was ushered in by the ringing of bells. This indeed was appropriate, that joyful sounds should herald a joyful event. Such public recognition sometimes is very effective, as it was in another

way two days before, when the flags were hung at half
mast on Good Friday.   From that hour a pall of darkness
hung over the world.   But now it seemed as if the world
began to breathe again, as this morning peal awoke the
echoes of the neighboring hills.   Listening, I thought how
joy answered to joy from one hill-top to another, from city
to city, and from land to land ; how the peal in Jerusalem
was answered by that in Rome ; and in every capital and
every cathedral, in a thousand temples, were repeated the
tidings of joy.   In Russia, in Moscow and St. Petersburg,
friends meeting in the streets rush into each other's arms,
embracing and exclaiming "The Lord is risen ! "   So does
this one event send joy to the ends of the world.

   With Easter the religious celebrations came to a close,
and immediately the pilgrims began to depart.   Passing the
Greek Convent, I saw a procession preparing for its homeward march.   The next morning the different companies,
representing different countries and Churches, were streaming over the hills ; while Cook's tourists, piled into waggons,
went rattling down the road to Jaffa.   The Holy Week
was ended. /

# CHAPTER V.

## A SOLITARY WALK FROM GETHSEMANE TO CALVARY.

/ If the services of Holy Week were all that Jerusalem had to offer, it would be hardly worth the while to cross the seas on a pilgrimage to the Holy City. As in Rome, so in Jerusalem, the form has killed the spirit, and services designed to recall the most tender scenes in the life of our Divine Master, are made the occasion of theatrical display. Such exhibitions may be entertaining, but they are not edifying ; we may have our curiosity excited and gratified, and yet at the same moment we are inexpressibly sadden- ed, at such caricatures of what we hold most sacred. The impression is that of any other dramatic spectacle : there is nothing that sinks into the mind and heart, to remain an assurance forever of the great realities here commemorated —nothing to make one a more believing disciple of Him who lived and died and rose again. Indeed if I were to end here, I should almost be of Mr. Spurgeon's opinion, that it were better to be content with the Life of Christ as we have it in the Gospels, than to try to reproduce it among the hills and valleys of Judea. /

And yet it is not to be inferred that there is nothing to

be found in Jerusalem that can minister to faith or to devotion. For this one needs to detach himself from the round of celebrations, from legends and traditions, and wander alone, with his New Testament in his hand, in the paths which his Master trod. Jerusalem in its surroundings is the same as it was two thousand years ago. The hills are all here. The mountains are round about Jerusalem as they were when David from his palace on Mount Zion cast his eye round the horizon, and found in their everlasting presence the emblem of God's faithfulness. And having gone thus far with the crowd of pilgrims to the great Festivals, perhaps my readers will be willing to accompany me when I take my walks about Jerusalem alone. /

The impressions of a traveller depend on a variety of causes, chief of which is his own temperament, or it may be some passing mood, whether he is gay or sad, buoyant with hope, or depressed by disappointment. The causes are wholly personal, and of interest to no one but himself. Yet these peculiar moods prepare him to receive peculiar impressions. Jerusalem is a very different place to him who comes burdened with a great sorrow, from what it is to him who comes in the lightness of heart of the ordinary traveller. Wherever one may go, he drags the past behind him : and all he sees is colored by his own secret thoughts and memories. Some years since I made a journey round the world, seeking relief from the oppression of a great sorrow. But I found that though a traveller may fly to the ends of the earth, he cannot escape from himself. Wherever I went, a shadow darkened every landscape, and an undertone of sadness mingled even with the voices of nature, with the singing of birds as well as the sighing of the wind or the moaning of the sea. When I reached the other hemisphere, it seemed as if the past must drop away (how could America touch me in the heart of Asia?) ; yet at Calcutta came the anniversary of the saddest event of my life, and in an instant all its*bitter memories came back again. Though a guest with friends, I could not bear even the lighted room or the cheerful company, but went out upon a balcony and sat for hours alone in the moonlight. All round the great city lay silent as if buried in slumber ; even the trees stood motionless in the breathless stillness of the tropical night : only the leaves of the palms were gently stirred by the evening wind. The Winter was but just over and gone, but already the fervid sun had brought the fulness of the Springtime, the season when De Quincey says that more than at any other we think of Death from its contrast with the fulness of life in nature : and

"As earth came forth with promise of the Spring,
I turned from all she brought to those she could not bring."

So finely is our whole being wrought and knit together, that it is impossible to separate the present from the past— the sight of what is from the memory of what has been :—

"And ever and anon there comes a wound
Striking the electric chord wherewith we are darkly bound."

In Jerusalem I felt no " wound," but only the touch of a hand : it was the most commonplace of all anniversaries— a birthday—which I mention only to show how slight a thing can give a turn to one's thoughts—how an event in one's own life, recurring in the midst of holy places, and causing personal memories to mingle with religious services, may strike the keynote of a whole week of musing and meditation. In truth it was a day to make one thoughtful, since it completed threescore years! It seemed as if with the touch of a hand there were the pointing of a finger to the long distance that had been passed on life's journey, and the shorter that yet remained.

It seemed to say, The day is far spent ; the sun is in the last quarter of the heavens, and hastens to his going down. Such thoughts do not make me sad, but they make me sober. Musing on all these vanished years, and the lives that had vanished with them, I was in no mood for crowds and shows, but rather for solitude and meditation. I did not feel that day like joining the throng of pilgrims, but rather like stealing away to some quiet spot where I could be alone. And what place so fit as that where the Master himself sought retirement? And so I went unto the Mount of Olives. Of the position of this sacred Mount there has never been a question : now, as in the time of our Saviour, it stands over against the city. Below was the bed of the Kedron, now dry as Summer dust, but which, at certain seasons of the year, after the early or the latter rain, is filled with a foaming torrent, that rises suddenly and as quickly disappears. What an image of human life! So swiftly does it pass away, and we are gone. ∫

The exact position of the Garden of Gethsemane is more of a question, although tradition, as usual, has fixed it with the utmost precision, marking its boundaries and enclosing it with a wall. The space within is laid out like a garden in the French style, with straight walks and trim hedges. The monk who showed us round plucked some leaves and flowers which we might carry away as mementoes of the sacred place. Fragrant as the spices which anointed Christ for burial were the flowers which bore a name so precious as that of the Garden of Gethsemane. Whether this be the very spot or no, it could not have been far away : for it was on the slope of Olivet ; somewhere on this hillside was the scene of that great agony. Even with the belittling attempt at landscape gardening, which gives to Gethsemane such a modern look, there is one feature which is ancient and venerable, in the olive-trees, gnarled and knotted like English oaks, which have stood here for centuries—some have said from the time of Christ. But this cannot be, for in the siege of Jerusalem by Titus, the trees were all cut down by the Tenth Legion. The present trees *may* date from the fourth century. Sitting down under them, we take out our New Testament and read the story of that night; how his sweat was, as it were, great drops of blood falling down to the ground as he prayed, "If it be possible, let this cup pass from me." When our Lord offered this prayer, he was within twenty-four hours of the end. He was about to descend into the Valley of the Shadow of Death, by the steps of unutterable humiliation: to be betrayed by one of his own disciples; to be seized by armed men; to be dragged to a Judgment Hall; to be mocked and scourged; and to be delivered up to the fury of his enemies. Who can think of such cruel sufferings of his Lord, without trying in some degree to drink in his spirit and imitate his example; to learn the hardest of all lessons—to bow his head, even in the midst of sorrow and pain, and say "Not my will, but thine be done"? /

Following the course of events of that mournful night, we returned to the city by St. Stephen's Gate, following the path along which our Lord was led by the Roman guard to Pilate's Hall. Of the points in Jerusalem that are determined, few are better known than the site of the Castle Antonia, Pilate's house and the Judgment Hall. Here was a scene which the masters have tried to depict. A great painting by a Hungarian artist recently attracted the attention of London and Paris, in which were very vividly portrayed the faces of that Jewish multitude, with their priestly leaders. In the judgment-seat sits the Roman Governor, whose command the attendant soldiers only wait to hear, but who is sorely puzzled what to decide. His head is bent in anxious thought ; he is trying to be rid of a case which troubles him—wishing to gratify the infuriated crowd which demands a sacrifice, and at the same time to clear himself of the guilt of shedding innocent blood. The face of Pilate is a masterpiece : but where the artist has failed—because he attempted the impossible—is in portraying the face of Christ ; yet even unsatisfactory as it is, there is a majesty in that countenance, unmoved except to sadness in the midst of the wild, tumultuous scene. Gustave Doré has attempted on a large canvas, to seize the moment of Christ's leaving the Pretorium, with the same result of a painting wonderful in its pictures of the different characters which compose the angry multitude, yet failing to give the Divine Form that moves serenely through them all to the great sacrifice. /

But little thought the disciples who watched that scene of its pictorial aspects. All idea of it as a spectacle was lost in the one overpowering thought of their Master's death. When the crowd issued from the Hall, fierce and exultant over its great victim, it took its course along a street which still bears the name of the Via Dolorosa. The ancient way is covered to a great depth by the débris of centuries ; but opposite the site of the Pretorium, under the Convent of the Sisters of Zion, have been found traces of the old Roman pavement, along which once rolled the chariots of Pilate and Herod ; and here it is not improbable that we tread the very stones that were pressed by the Saviour's feet, as he went forth bearing his cross. Tradition has attempted to designate every point in the Via Dolorosa, such as that where Jesus turned to the women who followed him, and "bewailed and lamented him," and said "Daughters of Jerusalem, weep not for me, but weep for yourselves and for your children"; and the spot where he fainted under his cross. We do not need to be thus precise. It is enough that we walk the Via Dolorosa in company with our Divine Master. What disciple can follow, even at this distance of time, a way filled with such memories, without saying to himself :

> " Must Jesus bear the cross alone,
> And all the world go free ?
> No ; there's a cross for every one,
> And there's a cross for me." /

And so following in all the way the Master trod in weariness and pain, we come at last to the site which tradition has fixed upon as Golgotha—the Place of a Skull. The place of crucifixion, like the place of burial, is included within the Church of the Holy Sepulchre, though it is at the other end of the church, in a recess, or chapel, by itself. As Golgotha is supposed to have been a rocky mound, which looked down on the garden at its foot, in which was the new sepulchre, the Chapel of the Crucifixion is at an elevation above the pavement, in a gallery, which is reached by a stair. I ascended the steps of stone, and at once saw by the altar at the end of the gallery, covered with votive offerings of gold and silver, which glistened in the light of the lamps suspended over it, that I was at the foot of Calvary. It is a sombre place, with a kind of sepulchral gloom, which the lights hung from the ceiling cannot dispel, as if the darkness of Death still lingered where the Lord expired. But Calvary is the centre which attracts all worshippers. As it was an interval in the services, the crowd had ebbed away ; only a few remained, who were held not so much by curiosity as by devotion. These were chiefly pilgrims of the humblest class. A woman whose countenance bore traces of a life of suffering, crept to the altar, and bowing, almost prostrating herself, kissed the spot where the cross stood. I have always observed that

those who come oftenest and linger longest, in such a place
of silence and meditation, are the poor in this world who
are rich in faith, to whom life is a burden heavy to be
borne, and to whom Religion is the only consolation.
Those to whom mere subsistence is a constant anxiety, find
comfort in looking up to him who had not where to lay
his head.   The aged and infirm come to one who, however
strong, does not repel their weakness.   Those who can
scarcely creep to the altar find support in looking to him
who bore our griefs and carried our sicknesses.   He who
comes for the last time, whom death has marked for its
own, finds strength in the sight of his dying Lord.   Even
the consciousness of sin does not keep away those who
come in penitence and confession to cast the load that
weighs heavy on the conscience, on him who bore our sins
in his own body on the tree.   Thus do all the types of
human infirmity—Poverty, and Sickness, and hoary Age ;
those who are broken with years and with sorrows ; kneel
together at the feet of him who is at once the Great
Sufferer and the Great Consoler. /

A spectacle so touching draws the coldest heart into
sympathy, and I could not look on unmoved.   Whatever
question I might have had as to the identity of the spot, I
was in no mood to raise that question now.   Here were
men and women on bended knees, in the full exercise of
faith and devotion ; and though I might not accept all that
they believed, yet recognizing the same great event, I bowed
my head, and in silent prayer joined with the worshippers.
And thus came into my heart a great peace.   Looking back,
I saw sixty years rolling away behind me, and felt no
regret at their departure.   They were gone ; let them go !
At the foot of the cross one learns to judge more justly of
life.   Things that once seemed great look very small.
How petty are our ambitions, our triumphs and our suc-/

cesses! Even our trials, which we love to magnify to exalt our courage and endurance, sink into nothing in the presence of our Saviour's agony. And so, at the foot of the cross, we gain strength to do and to suffer, to live and to die. Looking up into the face of Jesus Christ, we are answered by a look of infinite tenderness and compassion, which gives us a sense of protection and of safety. We are sure that "He who loved his own will love them unto the end." In all the rough way of life may He be with us! On this day of sober memories and anticipations, this is my prayer :

Abide with me! Fast falls the eventide;
The darkness deepens; Lord, with me abide!
When other helpers fail, and comforts flee,
Help of the helpless, oh abide with me!

Swift to its close ebbs out life's little day;
Earth's joys grow dim, its glories pass away;
Change and decay in all around I see:
O thou who changest not, abide with me!

. , . . . . . . . .

Hold thou thy cross before my closing eyes;
Shine through the gloom, and point me to the skies;
Heaven's morning breaks, and earth's vain shadows flee;
In life, in death, O Lord, abide with me! /

# CHAPTER VI.

## AT THE CROSS AND THE SEPULCHRE.

/ To come fully under the shadow of the cross, one visit to Calvary is not enough. I came and came again, and with each return to the sacred spot, the scene grew more real, and the moral effect grew deeper. Never can I forget my last visit the evening before I left Jerusalem. The Holy Week was ended, and the pilgrims had turned their faces towards home. Of course some still lingered, reluctant to depart ; but so few in comparison that one could walk the streets without being jostled by men wearing strange garbs and speaking strange tongues, and could visit the Church of the Holy Sepulchre and walk about undisturbed. It was nearly twilight when I descended into the court and passed under the old archway for the last time. What a contrast to the trampling crowds of the last week! The great church was empty. The stillness was almost painful ; and when, after awhile, there rose from a side chapel a vesper hymn—so soft and gentle was it, that like a distant echo, it seemed to add to the sense of silence that was otherwise unbroken. Thus all combined to produce the feeling of loneliness with which I ascended the stair, and came once more to the foot of Calvary.\

And is this the spot where my Saviour died ?   How can
I tell what others, far wiser and more learned, have tried
in vain to determine ?   Tradition affirms it, and even points
to the holes in the rock in which the three crosses stood.
If there were nothing but tradition to rest upon, that alone
would invest it with a sacred interest.   Here, where generations have knelt in adoration of their expiring Lord,
his death is more real and more present than on any other
spot of earth.   But there is at least a reasonable presumption that the tradition is founded on reality.   Underneath
the pavement is a rock which answers to the Mount of
Crucifixion.   Indeed one may reach down through an
opening in the marble floor, and thrust his hand into a
fissure which is said to have been caused by the earthquake, when "the rocks were rent and the graves were
opened."   None can deny that this *may* be the spot.   It is
at least possible that the disciples in the first centuries
kept the secret of the place, concealing it until it was safe
to mark it by an altar of worship.   If this be so, then am I
at this moment at the foot of the true Calvary, standing
where Mary stood—"Now there stood by the cross Mary
the mother of Jesus."   Of the Roman soldiers, it is said,
"And sitting down, they watched him there."   We too may
watch, silent and observant of that closing scene. /

To those who stood by the cross, the first impression
must have been that of intense physical suffering.   Crucifixion is one of the most painful forms of death which the
cruelty of man has been able to devise.   It is not instantaneous, but long and lingering, the sufferer sometimes
hanging for hours, with cords and nerves torn by the
nails, before death comes to his relief.   Nor had our
Master any of the alleviations which in some cases make
the suffering less intense.   In an old man, whose frame
has long been breaking, age that weakens the power of

action, also diminishes the capacity of suffering. Death comes easily to one who has anticipated it by a slow and gradual decay. But our Lord was in his early manhood— only thirty-three years old—with a body tenacious of life, and which took long to die. And so the hours which he hung upon the cross, must have been of an agony which can hardly be conceived. /

But to this were added other elements of suffering. The physical pain was nothing to the mental anguish. He suffered *alone:* for the malefactors who died with him but gave additional ignominy and bitterness to his death. Their presence was no solace to the dying Lord, nor had he any other. Martyrs have been followed to the scaffold or the stake by those who have kept up their courage by sympathy and admiration. But of such support Jesus had none. In all the city of Jerusalem, crowded as it was at the Feast of the Passover, few thought of him. His disciples "forsook him and fled." Even when they saw him led forth to execution, they followed only "afar off." A few faithful women, whom love inspired with courage, crept nearer to the foot of the cross. But how little could their love and devotion do for the Great Sufferer! For to this depth of anguish there was a still lower deep : not only was he deserted by men, but, as it seemed, forsaken by God. Was there ever a cry so bitter as that when there was darkness over all the land from the sixth to the ninth hour : "My God! my God! why hast thou forsaken me?" The heavens above were black ; there was not a gleam of light in all the horizon. In this darkened universe his spirit seemed to be passing into eternal night. Here was a source of anguish into which the beholders could not enter. Had the disciples clung to him ever so closely, they might indeed have proved their fidelity, but they could not have taken from the weight of that immense suffering. They could not touch the mighty wound. Not only could they not relieve it, they could not even comprehend it. Jesus Christ, when giving his life for the sins of the world, was beyond the reach of human sympathy. He trod the wine-press alone. /

So far as the sufferings of Christ were of the nature of a propitiation ; of an atonement for sin ; they were too great and awful to furnish an example for us. But as there was in him a mingling of the human and the divine, so in his sufferings there was much which answers to our own, and which we may learn to bear more patiently by looking to him.

The great want of the human heart is sympathy and affection, and in this Christ was a man, not only with all human sensibilities, but with cravings far more intense than ours. And yet in this world he was alone—alone while he lived and alone when he died. Some who have made a study of the physical cause of Christ's death, have said that he died of a broken heart. If so, it was mental suffering joined to the tension and laceration of the cross, which burst a heart that embraced a world in its boundless love. /

In this element of solitariness, our trials, small as they are, yet faintly resemble those of our Master. Do we tread the wilderness of this world alone ? So did he. Does the world care little for us? It cared little for him. Are we of small account in its esteem ? So was he. What can we suffer from want of companionship or sympathy compared with him, who was in the world, and the world was made by him, and the world knew him not ? Jesus drank the cup of humiliation to the very dregs, that he might be able to sympathize with the humblest of mankind. The mass of men are poor, but who so poor as he ? Do we ever think what honor our Lord put upon poverty by coming into the world in a condition so lowly? We might almost say that he could not have been the Redeemer of the world if he had not himself been poor : for he would have been far above the plane of ordinary human condition, and outside the pale of human sympathy. A profound distinction has been made between the Old Dispensation and the New : that while the former glorified prosperity, making it a proof of the favor of God that a man was rich in worldly possessions, in flocks and herds, the New glorifies adversity, making it rather a sign of the Divine favor that a man is chastened and brought low. It blesses the poor. This suits better the condition of the mass of mankind. To the greater part of the human race life is a disappointment. The more we aspire to that which is high, the more we suffer from being brought down to that which is low. Deep hidden within the breast are the pangs of wounded pride and disappointed ambition ; *but they are there.* The keenest sting to our pride in our contests with the world, is to have the wicked triumph over us ; to be overcome by the mean and the malignant ; to hear their laugh of scorn, their cruel mockery, in the hour of defeat. Yet Christ was humbled in the presence of his enemies ; he was pursued with relentless hatred ; he was brought to the scaffold. It was at that moment, when dying from the malice of his persecutors, that he prayed "Father, forgive them, for they know not what they do "—an abnegation of self so complete that it drew from the great French writer of the last century, Rousseau, this confession : " Socrates died like a philosopher, but Jesus Christ like a God!" If God could forgive such crimes, cannot we forgive our petty injuries? Should not such forgiveness draw out of our hearts every feeling of hatred and bitterness? Is there any abasement of our pride that is not easy to bear when we contemplate the voluntary humiliation of the Greatest among men? Shall the disciple be greater than his Master, or the servant greater than his Lord? \

But there are some that have no ambition and no pride, and yet are fearfully alone. To such the Master comes in the deepest solitude, and by his coming takes away the feeling of desolateness. His sympathy is so delicate and tender, so mindful of human infirmity, so gentle and forgiving, that it glides into the heart and steals away its sorrow. Who can be lonely with such a Friend and Companion? Though one climb the highest mountain, Christ is there. Though he sail the farthest ocean, even there, in the darkness of midnight, he can see a Form walking on the waves, and hear a voice saying "It is I; be not afraid." So Christ comes to us in our darkest night, in our extremest need; in what seems to us utter loneliness. He who was himself deserted of men; whose life was so solitary; can comfort all the lonely. There is not a heart so desolate, nor a life so dreary, into which his presence cannot bring an ineffable peace. And not only will he be with us in the loneliness of life, but in the loneliness of death: for then it is that we are most solitary, when we venture forward into the dark and the unknown. In the Church of Rome, when one is near his end, the priest comes to the bedside, and holds up the crucifix before the eyes, and presses it to the lips, of the dying, that the sight of his Lord may give him strength to pass through the gates of death. We use no such symbols, but coming to the foot of the cross, even the sternest Protestant must bow his head and say, Jesus, look on me! For such prayer this is the place. Its associations make a Real Presence of the body and blood of Christ. We seem to look up into the Master's face, and to hear his voice saying "Son, Daughter, go in peace; thy sins are forgiven thee!" He who looked down from the height of his cross, and spoke words of comfort to the weeping group at his feet, comforts us also. He who forgave His enemies, forgives our ingratitude, and gives us peace.

If it were not too much dividing our thoughts, one would be tempted here to trace the Cross in History, and mark the revolutions of time ; to note how the instrument of torture and of ignominy has become a sign of glory—a badge worn in the crowns of emperors and kings, and a sign lifted up on the spires of great capitals ; to observe how an influence starting from this spot, like a fountain bursting from the rock, has flowed through history—the purifying element of all modern civilization. Looking at it in these general bearings, so vast and remote, one may well use the language of exultation :

> " In the Cross of Christ I glory,
>     Towering o'er the wrecks of Time;
> All the lights of ancient story
>     Gather round that head sublime."/

But one who comes to the foot of Calvary is not in a mood to philosophize upon history. This little chapel is but a small oratory compared with the great cathedrals of Christendom ; but it is the spot where, according to tradition, the Crucifixion took place, and that gives it an interest which does not belong to all the cathedrals in the world. As a Christian stands here at the foot of the cross, he is thinking, not of the relation of his Master's death to the world, but to his own soul—to him as one who has to live and to die, and to go to the bar of judgment ; and the utterance of his heart is " God be merciful to me, a sinner ! "—" Lord, remember me when thou comest into thy kingdom ! "/

From the Chapel of the Crucifixion, I descended to the floor of the church, pausing at the stone which marks the spot where the body was anointed for burial, and came to the place of the Sepulchre. When I had been here before, the Latin fathers were standing in front of it, some of whom were stalwart men, with rich deep voices, and sang in triumphant strains the glorious Hymns of the Resurrection. Now all was still as I went down the steps alone, and entered the place of entombment. This, though called a chapel, is no bigger than a monk's cell, and one has to do almost as did the disciples, Peter and John—to "stoop down" in order to enter it. It is indeed a "narrow house," but it is enough ; it is sufficient for a tomb. Here was the new sepulchre, wherein was never man laid till it received the body of our Lord. The old rock-sepulchre is not here. There may have been a cavity hollowed out below, in which the body was laid ; but if so, it is covered from sight by slabs of marble, in form like a sarcophagus, whereon, as an altar, the mass is celebrated daily, according to the rites of both the Greek and the Latin Church— "an unbloody offering," as it is called, for the quick and dead. /

What interest gathers and is focused in this hallowed spot, the very centre of Christendom—of its faith and devotion! Within these narrow walls what prayers have been offered, and what tears have been shed! What a place for memories, for sorrows, and for hopes! A world of memories came sweeping through the mind, as a lightning flash reveals a whole landscape that is buried in darkness—thoughts of the dead lying in graves far off beyond the sea. As I knelt and bowed my head on the cold stone, it seemed as if I laid both head and heart upon a coffin lid which had suddenly closed on a beloved form and face. Within were the eyes that shone, and the lips that spoke to ours, but that would not look or speak again. We listen, if we may not hear the deep-drawn breath or the beating of the heart ; but no sound escapes : the lips are sealed, the heart is still, the hands are folded on the breast. So have come generations of the broken-hearted, and poured out their tears on the tomb of the Crucified. Here kings and emperors, with millions of every rank and of forty or fifty generations, have knelt and prayed, and sobbed and wept, for those who were gone not to return. Well might they weep when standing within the portals of the tomb, in the presence of a reality which cannot be disguised. Cover the coffin with flowers, bury it with wreaths and garlands—that does not change the awful fact of DEATH. The life that was is ended; is there another life to begin? For that, the resurrection of Christ is our only hope. Abstract arguments for the immortality of the soul, amount to little. At best they enable us only to say with the ancient philosophers, "We hope rather than believe." But if out of this sepulchre there has been a return of One from the unnumbered dead, that is a pledge of the resurrection of all. This is the turning-point of our Faith and our Religion. What mighty hopes hang upon the single fact of the Resurrection! "If Christ be not risen, then they that are fallen asleep in Christ are perished. But now is Christ risen from the dead!" The answer to all skepticism is this: "If we believe that Christ died and rose again, even so them also which sleep in Jesus will God bring with him."/

As I came out of the Chapel of the Sepulchre, it seemed as if I were coming out of a tomb. When I left the church, the shades of evening had fallen, and the gathering darkness reminded me of another night that was fast coming on, in which no man can work. I had just passed a milestone on my life's journey, and was a year's march nearer to the grave. But I had found strength for the inevitable hour. I had been to the place where the Lord lay, and had seen the stone rolled away from the door of the sep-

ulchre, and seen a vision of angels who said that He was
alive. I hastened through the streets as in a dream—as if
I had been one of the army of the dead laid to sleep in
Jerusalem centuries ago, that had crept out of the tomb,
and was now fleeing like an affrighted ghost. And that
night, as I sat once more on the balcony, which was my
place of meditation, and looked up at the ancient Tower
of David, around which Jew and Roman, Turk and Crusader, had fought, and under whose shadow all lie buried
together, how little a thing seemed human life beside the
monuments which man himself had builded! Men come
and go, but these stand fast like the everlasting hills.
This was my last night in Jerusalem ; to-morrow I should
depart to return no more. But my pilgrimage had not
been in vain, since in revisiting the scenes of our Lord's
life and death and resurrection, I had found my faith
strengthened in the Divine reality. Never had I so felt
how comprehensive was that Creed—so brief, so simple,
and yet so sublime—which has been repeated for generations :

I BELIEVE IN GOD, THE FATHER ALMIGHTY, MAKER OF HEAVEN
AND EARTH ;

AND IN JESUS CHRIST, HIS ONLY SON, OUR LORD, WHO WAS
CONCEIVED BY THE HOLY GHOST, BORN OF THE VIRGIN MARY,
SUFFERED UNDER PONTIUS PILATE, WAS CRUCIFIED, DEAD, AND
BURIED. THE THIRD DAY HE ROSE FROM THE DEAD. HE ASCENDED
INTO HEAVEN, AND SITTETH ON THE RIGHT HAND OF GOD, THE
FATHER ALMIGHTY. . . .

I BELIEVE . . . IN THE LIFE EVERLASTING.

It is enough : in the strength of that great hope will I
take up my pilgrim's staff for the rest of my journey. The
future is dark before me, but not with unknown terrors.
Welcome the twilight! welcome the shadows! since
beyond the darkness shines the light of Eternal Day. /

# CHAPTER VII.

## LEAVING JERUSALEM—TO BETHEL, SHILOH, AND JACOB'S WELL.

/ At length the time had come when we must leave Jerusalem. For eleven days we had been going round about her walls, marking her towers and bulwarks, and musing in her desolate places. The impression had been sad and mournful. We had seen the Jews wailing at the foundation stones of the ancient temple, and again celebrating the Passover, as if in all their sorrow and humiliation, they would keep the memory of their ancient deliverance, and hope for a brighter future for their country and their race. And with the mosque of the Moslem and the synagogue of the Jew, we had seen with far deeper interest the places associated with the life and death of our Blessed Lord.

Rich with such memories, we were now to leave the holy city and turn our steps northward, through Samaria and Galilee, to Shechem and Nazareth, to the Mount of the Beatitudes and the shores of the Lake of Galilee, to Damascus, and to the glory of Hermon and of Lebanon. /

But a new journey required a fresh preparation. On arriving at Jerusalem, we had given up our attendants, not thinking that dignity required that we should keep our tents standing without the gates, with all the retainers of a camp, while we were lodged at a hotel. Accordingly we had parted with Yohanna, the dragoman who had conducted us from the Red Sea across the desert to Mount Sinai, and from Sinai to Jerusalem. After a few days Dr. Post had been obliged to return to Beirut, and I was left alone. In making new arrangements, I was happy to fall once more among mine own countrymen. There were a number of Americans in Jerusalem, among them the Rev. Dr. Adams of Fall River, Mass., who with his wife had been for some months travelling in Europe and the East. We had met in Florence and Rome and Naples, from which we sailed together for Alexandria. We parted at Cairo (they going up the Nile, while I crossed the desert), and met again at Jerusalem, with mutual congratulations that we might now make a journey through the Holy Land together. Dr. Adams had known Dr. Post in the Union Theological Seminary, New York. I counted it extremely fortunate that since I had lost the one as a travelling companion, I could have the other; while the presence of an American lady gave to our tent-life not a little of the sweet sense of home. /

With them was a young theological student, a Mr. Weeden, who was to share my tent ; and an English gentleman and his wife. The party had been made up by Dr. Adams, who had engaged as dragoman Mr. Rolla Floyd of Jaffa, who is well known in Palestine, where he was for many years in charge of Cook's excursion parties. A few months before they had "fallen out" on some matter of business, which I never understood, and of which it is not worth while to repeat the gossip of Jerusalem. Their difference did not concern us ; our wish was to obtain the best possible guide to Palestine, and that we believed

we had found in Mr. Floyd.  He is an American, who
went to Jaffa years ago with a colony from Maine, of which
he is the only remaining representative.  After the colony
was broken up, instead of returning to America, he stayed
in Jaffa, and became a guide and dragoman to travellers.
He is a man of great intelligence, especially in all matters
which concern the geography and the historical and Biblical associations of the Holy Land.  He has the Bible at
his tongue's end, and can quote chapter and verse for any
place to which he comes, from one end of the country to
the other.  At the same time he is a man of splendid
physique, of great physical strength and courage—quali-
ties not to be left out of account in one who has to conduct
a party, to keep the upper hand of quarrelsome muleteers,
as well as a sharp lookout against the thieves who infest
almost every village, certainly every favorite camping
ground of travellers.  He took entire charge of the expedi-
tion, engaging horses and mules and muleteers, and providing the tents which were to be for several weeks our
" house and home." * /

* My attention was first called to Mr. Floyd by the Hon. S. S.
Cox, the well known Member of Congress, whom I met in Paris,
as he was returning from a brief tour in the Holy Land.  For the
benefit of travellers who may yet have the same tour to make,
I quote the following from Rev. Joseph Cook :

After eight years' acquaintance with my American country-
man, Rolla Floyd, I regard him as incomparably the most accomplished, efficient, and in every way trustworthy conductor of travel
in Palestine and Syria.  I travelled in the Holy Land under his
advice in 1873, and under his personal guidance with my wife in
1881.  All my prolonged and varied experience with Mr. Floyd
has convinced me of the entire justice of the really unmeasured
commendation which it is well known has been heaped upon him
by hundreds of travellers whom he has conducted through the
Holy Land, and especially by the London firm of Cook's Tourist
Agency, of which he was the foremost representative in Palestine

With such preparations, we mustered on the morning of the 11th of April at an inn without the gate on the Jaffa road. Half an hour was spent in trying the horses that were to carry us. Each one of the party mounted several and tried their paces, and when each had made his selection, saddles had to be adjusted, till at last all were satisfied, and we began slowly and deliberately our long journey. /

Hardly were we in the saddle before we dismounted at the Tombs of the Kings, which are but a short distance without the city walls. The ancient Jews, like the Egyptians (from whom perhaps they derived the custom), paid great honor to their dead, as we see in the Tombs of the Judges and the Tombs of the Prophets. Indeed their honor to the dead was sometimes greater than their respect for the authority of the living. Christ rebukes them for their hypocrisy in "building the tombs of the prophets, and garnishing the sepulchres of the righteous," when their conduct showed that they were "the children of them which killed the prophets." Whether these Tombs of the Kings be really the place where the monarchs of

and Syria for seven years. This firm has often eulogized in the strongest language in its official pamphlets and periodicals his honesty, courage, intelligence, skill and success as a conductor of travel. It has pointed with pride to his knowledge of the Holy Land, his extraordinary familiarity with Scriptural allusions to the sacred places, his perfect command of the Arabic language, and the universal esteem in which he is held by the Arabs, and even by the Bedaween tribes. Acting now as an independent conductor of travel, Mr. Floyd is sometimes treated by powerful tourist agencies as a dangerous rival. It remains true, however, that the commendations just cited are thoroughly deserved, and that his eleven years of experience as a guide has made him unsurpassable in his department. I take pleasure in commending him to the visitors of the Holy Land, and I write this testimonial without his solicitation.     JOSEPH COOK (Boston).

Jaffa, Palestine, Dec. 15, 1881. /

Judah and of Israel were laid, is uncertain ; but at least
here was a grand mausoleum. Descending a broad flight
of steps, we find ourselves in a large court, which opens
into numerous side chambers, where successive kings were
laid in their royal house of death. Alas, that such a vast
subterranean temple, chiselled out of the solid rock, could
not keep their dust. The tombs are tenantless, the sepulchres are empty—even the very names of those who once
slept here are unknown. Such is the fate of the greatest
as well as the least of those who are born to die. It is not
only " dust to dust," but dust to oblivion.

A little farther on our way, we reached the top of
Scopus, that broad plateau on which Titus camped with
his army for the fatal siege. Here we reined in our horses,
and turned to take a last look at Jerusalem. We could
not see it very clearly, as a wind from the sea had blown
up a mist which hung over the city ; yet we could trace
the line of the walls by the towers which rose above them,
and which were surmounted in turn by the Mosque of
Omar, as we had often seen the mightier dome of St. Paul's
towering through the cloud that hangs over London. And
thus, while we gazed with lingering eyes, the vision seemed
to fade away like a phantom city, and with it our last
sight of the earthly Jerusalem. /

Turning to pursue our journey, we have an opportunity
to survey our party as it stretches along the line of march.
All are mounted on horses, except the English lady, who
not being strong enough to undertake a three weeks' ride,
is carried in a palanquin, a huge affair, borne by two
mules. If we had had a broad and level road before us, it
might have been swung between them, as a sort of ham-
mock is sometimes swung between two camels on the
desert. But the bridle-paths of Palestine are quite too
narrow for two mules, or two horses, or even two small

donkeys, to go abreast.    So one of the mules is harnessed
in front, while the other comes behind.    They are huge
creatures, large and strong, as they need to be to support
such a load, going up and down the rocky hills of Palestine.
The palanquin is very cumbrous and awkward ; but the
lady who sits in it says that it is not uncomfortable ; while
its very hugeness gives an air of grandeur and dignity to our
whole party.    Gathered round such a " chariot," we who are
outriders, feel as if we were a royal escort, attending the
Queen of Sheba on her way to pay a visit to King Solomon.

There is nothing like imagination to give a touch of
majesty to one's goings, and convert an ordinary ride into
a royal progress.    Sitting erect on my Syrian steed, I fancy
myself a Crusader taking the field for the recovery of the
Holy Sepulchre, and whisper *sotto voce* the opening line of
Spenser's Fairy Queen :

"A gentle knight came pricking o'er the plain "

—a description which applies perfectly to the present
rider, except that he is *not* " a gentle knight " ; that " the
plain " is a succession of rough hills ; and that instead of
" pricking over " them, we rarely go out of a walk.    With
these exceptions, the resemblance is complete ; though it
is reduced pretty much to this, that, like the " gentle
knight," I am mounted on horseback, and riding in the
land of the Crusaders. /

If our march be slow, so much the better opportunity
does it give to observe the country and study the physical
geography of Palestine.    The best substitute for personal
observation is a good " raised map," which gives the mountains in relief, with the great depression of the Jordan and
the Dead Sea.    A glance will show how Palestine is divided
by a mountain ridge, which forms the backbone of the
country.    This ridge is seamed and scarred throughout its

whole length, and its sides cut into ravines, through which a hundred streams, from the pouring of the annual rains, run off to the Jordan and the Dead Sea on one side, or the Mediterranean on the other. As the hills are all of stratified limestone, the rains which have denuded them of vegetation have laid bare the rocks, and given them a very desolate appearance. At this season of the year—the month of April—this desolation is relieved by the innumerable wild flowers which deck the hillsides, and the harvests which are ripening in the valleys between : for it is now "the time of barley-harvest."/

But if the country were ever so cheerless, its associations clothe it with a majesty that is more attractive than grand scenery or brilliant vegetation. As we turned away from Jerusalem, and began to look round the horizon, the most commanding object to the West was the ancient hill of Mizpeh (a noble height, three thousand feet above the sea), which from the earliest times was a watch-tower from which the Hebrew sentinels surveyed not only the Plain of Sharon at its foot, but the whole country from Hebron to Mount Carmel, and from the Mediterranean to the mountains of Moab—a summit which takes its present name, Neby Samwill, from the tradition that makes it at once the birth-place and the burial-place of the prophet Samuel. Here Saul came to him, and was chosen by him, and anointed to be King of Israel ; and here he mustered " all the children of Israel " " from Dan to Beersheba, with the land of Gilead " (which is beyond the Jordan), presenting an array of " four hundred thousand men that drew sword." Such are the stirring memories that gather round these hoary summits, which, as they come upon us to-day, seem to cast mighty shadows on the mountains, like the flying clouds which are at this moment rolling upward from the Mediterranean. /

As we continued our journey we passed parties of pilgrims who had come up to Jerusalem to witness the services of Holy Week, and now were returning to their homes, just as the ancient Jews returned from keeping the Passover. In such a company often was found the Saviour himself, passing over this very road, which is the road to Nazareth. Indeed, one of the places through which we passed, Beeroth, a town in Benjamin, where we stopped to take our midday rest, is designated by tradition (which must find a site for every incident in sacred story) as that where Joseph and Mary first missed from the caravan the wonderful child, and returned to Jerusalem to find him in the Temple disputing with the doctors.

Other names of hamlets remind us that we are passing over places familiar in the Old Testament, such as Nob and Gibbeah, and Ataroth and Rock Rimmon. Just now we are riding through Ramah, and instantly recurs that most pathetic passage : "In Rama was there a voice heard, lamentation and weeping, and great mourning, Rachel weeping for her children, and would not be comforted, because they are not." As we think of the bereaved mother, the whisperings of sorrow seem still to rise from the ground that has been wet with her tears, and to fill the air that has trembled with the voice of her lamentation.

This region is full of patriarchal memories. Do you see that hill yonder, rising on the opposite side of a soft green valley ? That is Bethel—the very spot where Abraham, when a wanderer "journeying towards the South," "pitched his tent," and "builded an altar unto the Lord" (Genesis xii. 8), and to which Jacob returned as a place of holy visitations, and casting himself on the ground, with a stone for a pillow, saw a ladder whose top reached to heaven, and the angels of God ascending and descending upon it. It were easy to make light of these sacred associ-

ations, especially when we see such hallowed places dese-
crated by a wretched village and a miserable population.
But to a devout mind, whose thoughts are far away on
times long gone, there is an inspiration in the thought that
this very ground has been touched by angels' feet ; that
here on this rocky height, the patriarch, choosing one of
its stones on which to rest his weary head, fell asleep, and
to his closed eyes there came the heavenly vision. May
we not find in the wanderings of that ancient pilgrim, a
type of our own wanderings through this world, and pray
that in our loneliness, in the darkness of the night, we may
catch some glimpse of an opened heaven, and so be
brought nearer to God :

> " Though like the wanderer,
>   The sun gone down,
> Darkness be over me,
>   My rest a stone,
> Yet in my dreams I'd be
> Nearer, my God, to thee,
>   Nearer to thee.

Continuing our journey, we passed over a rugged country, sometimes riding on the very crest of the hills, and
then descending into valleys green with the freshness of
the early Spring, which were all the more beautiful from
contrast with the rocky hillsides. The constant ascents
and descents, and windings here and there, gave a pleasant variety to our ride, which made us forget the rough-
ness of the path beneath our feet. Some of the valleys
were mere dells, whose narrowness, so closely were they
shut in by the hills, was unpleasantly suggestive of such
interruptions to the pleasure of travel as befell the man
who went down to Jericho, for indeed nothing is easier
than to " fall among thieves." Just here, where a rising
cliff offers a grateful shade from the afternoon sun, and the

water trickling down the face of the rock is as cooling as if dripping from "the moss-covered bucket that hangs in the well," it adds to the charm of the secluded spot to be reminded that this is the famous Robbers' Fountain, near which several caves offer convenient hiding places from which they might spring out on the unsuspecting traveller. However, we rode on with no interruption, receiving only pleasant salutations from the people in the villages or at work in the fields, or the pilgrims who were keeping their homeward march.

As it drew towards evening, we turned from our forward course and rode up a hillside to the little hamlet of Sinjil, where we halted at a well known camping ground for travellers.  We were not surprised that parties liked to camp there, for the situation is beautiful—on a hill-top which commands a wide outlook over the country.  Here we pitched our tents near the village, whose neighborhood might give us a sense of protection—the first thing to be thought of in travelling through Palestine.  Hardly were the horses unsaddled and picketed before the dragoman sent to the head-man of the village for a guard to make us safe against marauders, to which he received the pleasing answer that the appointed "guardians of the peace" were "unavoidably detained," for the reason that he had sent guards for two parties before us, both of which had found the temptation so great, that instead of keeping off thieves, they had turned robbers themselves, for which they had been arrested and thrown into prison!  Indeed, to confess the whole truth, he had been so unfortunate that a dozen of his faithful servants were now in jail at Nablous for making too free with the property of travellers.  Being thus deprived of our "natural protectors," the dragoman was obliged to fall back on his own trusty revolvers.  He took out his brace of six-barrelled pistols, to see that they were loaded, and sticking them in his belt, sent word to the sheikh that he intended to stand guard himself, and advised him to look out that none of his thievish rascals came within range. The hint was not lost : not a mouse stirred. True, the muleteers passed an anxious night, as they had to alternate in watches ; while poor Floyd slept with one eye open, or rather did not sleep at all. But thanks to such protection, we slept as tranquilly as if we had been in a quiet New England village.

But whatever the watchings or the dangers of the night, the rising sun drove away all such thoughts, as it dispelled the mists that rose up from the valley below, and we were soon in the saddle, " pricking " over the hills and winding through the valleys with exquisite delight.

Already in a single day's journey we had been in the territory of three of the Jewish tribes. Starting from that of Judah, we had passed through "the lot of Benjamin," and entered into the larger and broader territory of Ephraim, the central region of Palestine, and one of remarkable fertility. In the allotments to the different tribes, a special inheritance fell to the house of Joseph. When Jacob called his sons around his deathbed, to tell them what should befall them in the last days, he said : " Joseph is a fruitful bough by a well, whose branches run over the wall. The archers have sorely grieved him, and shot at him, and hated him. But his bow abode in strength, and the arms of his hands were made strong by the hands of the mighty God of Jacob " ; and then foretold for him and his descendants great temporal prosperity as the reward of filial love—a benediction which is repeated in the words of the dying Moses :

And of Joseph he said, Blessed of the Lord be his land, for the precious things of heaven, for the dew, and for the deep that coucheth beneath,

And for the precious fruits brought forth by the sun, and for the precious things put forth by the moon,

And for the chief things of the ancient mountains, and for the precious things of the lasting hills,

And for the precious things of the earth and fulness thereof, and for the good will of him that dwelt in the bush : let the blessing come upon the head of Joseph, and upon the top of the head of him that was separated from his brethren.

His glory is like the firstling of his bullock, and his horns are like the horns of unicorns : with them he shall push the people together to the ends of the earth : and they are the ten thousands of Ephraim, and they are the thousands of Manasseh.

Of course the glory of that ancient time has passed away, but something of the beauty of Ephraim lingers still in these hills and valleys. Many of the hillsides, through which the strata of rock crop out here and there, are cultivated ; the remains of old terraces still bear orchards of olives and fig trees ; while the valleys remind us of that South Country which so enchanted us as we came up out of the desert. Nor is Ephraim wanting in ancient and sacred associations. On the contrary it is much older than Judah. Our ride this morning led across a fertile plain, on which rose a gentle eminence marked by some old ruins. This was SHILOH, the very centre of the first Hebrew State, where the Tabernacle was set up and the Ark of the Lord was kept hundreds of years before the building of the Temple. Here the tribes gathered as in later times at Jerusalem. Here lived the prophet Eli till he was nearly a hundred years old, when he fell at the tidings that the Ark of God was taken. What interest gathers round these ancient altars ! How they tell the story of an age when the religion was the government, and the prophet a judge. "He had judged Israel forty years." This spot links together two periods of Jewish history—Eli, the last of the Judges, with Samuel, who grew up at his feet, and who anointed Saul, the first of the line of Kings.

Other sacred scenes rose in sight before the day was over. About noon we came out upon a hill-top which commanded a view for many miles up the great plain of Mukhna, where Jacob fed his flocks, with Mount Gerizim in the distance. Pursuing our way in the afternoon, we came to Sychar, "where was a well" which was dug by father Jacob himself, and where more than seventeen hundred years later Jesus sat and talked to the woman of Samaria.

Here we dismounted, and sat down by the well, which had such sacred memories. There was at first a feeling of disappointment to find it a neglected spot. Its desolate appearance makes some almost regret to have seen it, while others keep away lest the sight should be even painful, as it dispelled their hallowed associations. In the conversation with Mr. Spurgeon, to which I have referred, he said with a good deal of vehemence that "nothing could induce him to visit the Holy Land," in support of which he related the experience of a friend (I think an American clergyman) on this very spot, to which he had come as a holy place, thinking how he would "sit on the well," as his Master did, and taking out his Bible, read again the beautiful story of Christ's conversation with the woman of Samaria, musing on the wonderful scene with tender emotion. But, said Mr. Spurgeon, when he came to the spot, he found it neglected and desolate, and his devout meditations interrupted by a crowd of importunate beggars, clamoring for backsheesh! This was a dismal prospect to set before a traveller just starting for the East, "going bound in the spirit unto Jerusalem." But our experience was more fortunate. We had no annoyance. To be sure, the place is neglected. But that mattered little; it would not have helped the impression if we had come upon a spring abundant as that of Elisha at Jericho, ont!

bubbling up in a marble fountain. Here was nothing but an old well—old indeed, for it was dug by our father Jacob more than three thousand years ago. This is one of the few spots in Palestine whose identity is almost certain, and which is therefore truly venerable. It is not the well of Herod, or of any of the Roman conquerors, but of one whose very name gave it a sacredness even before the time of Christ, and to which he came as a hallowed spot. Here the patriarch lived with all his sons around him, save one whom he supposed to be dead, but who had been sold into captivity and carried down to Egypt, and there risen to power, to be in time the savior of his father's house. To that long-lost son, in memory of his filial devotion, Jacob gave this very plot of ground on which we are now standing, and in which, two hundred years after his death, his body was laid. There are few more touching illustrations of a love strong in death—the love of one's early home, such as to make him desire to be buried near the spot where he was born—than the last command of Joseph. He was about to die—to die in Egypt, amid all the splendor of the court of Pharaoh. But at that moment his thoughts were not on the banks of the Nile; they wandered back to the scenes of his childhood, to the time when he had been a shepherd's boy and kept his father's flock; and calling his brethren around him, he said "I die; but God will surely visit you, and bring you out of this land unto the land which he sware to Abraham, to Isaac, and to Jacob. And Joseph took an oath of the children of Israel, saying God will surely visit you, and ye shall carry up my bones from hence. So Joseph died, being an hundred and ten years old; and they embalmed him, and he was put in a coffin in Egypt." But there he was not to remain. When came the time of the Exodus of the Israelites, his bones were taken with pious care, and carried with them in all their marches, till finally laid to rest in this very piece of ground, which his father Jacob bought for a portion for him.

Joseph's Tomb is but a short distance from Jacob's Well, into which we are now looking down. The top has been partly arched over, covering a little space around what we should call the "curb" of the well. The dragoman gave me his strong arm, and lifting me over this upper and outer rim, let me down a few feet to a point from which I got a nearer view of the depth below. Explorers who have measured it have found it over a hundred feet deep, but a part of this has been filled up by the stones cast into it.

But how came Jacob to dig such a well? is a question often asked. He was close to the Vale of Shechem, which is full of streams. What need of boring a hundred feet through the solid rock to find what a mile or two distant was running away in exhaustless abundance? The answer is that neighbors are not always friends; that the inhabitants of the towns and the shepherds of the plains had little to do with each other, and even might be in open feud. In the time of Christ "the Jews had no dealings with the Samaritans," and seventeen hundred years before the progenitor of the Hebrew race may have been to them a stranger and an alien. The people of Shechem might be friendly to-day, and enemies to-morrow ; and though they might have water flowing through their city, they might at any moment shut it off from him. With all his flocks and herds, he could not be dependent on such an uncertain supply. And so he dug this well, "and drank thereof himself, and his children, and his cattle." The woman of Samaria, who came here to draw water, had probably been out on the plain tending the flocks, and at the sixth hour —noon—had no other spring to go to but Jacob's Well.

But the chief interest of this spot is that One greater than Jacob or Joseph has been here. On this very ground, sitting where we now sit, our Saviour sat, and talked with the woman of Samaria, revealing to her astonished eyes that in the worship of God the place matters little ; that "neither in this mountain," looking up to. Gerizim which rose above them, "nor yet at Jerusalem," shall men "worship the Father": for that " God is a spirit, and they that worship him must worship him in spirit and in truth."

With such thoughts of the Great Master, whose presence has touched all these heights and valleys with a glory like that of the setting sun, which now gilds the tops of Ebal and Gerizim, we mounted our horses and rode through the narrow valley which separates them, and passing round the town, camped under some old olive trees at its western end, at the foot of Mount Gerizim. We were now in Nablous, the ancient Shechem. As our visit here was somewhat full of incident, it is worthy of a fuller description.

# CHAPTER VIII.

NABLOUS—A DAY THAT WAS NOT ALL SUNSHINE—
A TALE OF ROBBERY AND OF TURKISH JUSTICE.

In " wandering through the wilderness of this world,"
I have had varied experiences—days that were bright and
days that were dark, and days that were both bright and
dark, cloud and sunshine following each other in quick
succession. But not many days have I had anywhere the
experience of which was so far from previous expectation,
as that we spent in the ancient city of Nablous. As we
entered the valley, there was something in the very atmosphere which revived us. We were greeted with the sound
of running streams (there are said to be seventy springs
issuing from the hills), which rush joyously through the
valley. We were entering a city of Samaria whose history
goes back to the time of the Captivity, when the Ten
Tribes were carried away to Assyria, and earlier still, to
the days when Jacob fed his flocks on the adjacent plain.
We had come up from Jacob's Well, the place where our
Lord had been, and passed between Mount Ebal and
Mount Gerizim, from which it seemed as if alternate blessing and cursing rolled over our heads. And now we were
camped at the foot of Gerizim, the mount of blessing, the
very clouds of which ought to rain perpetual benediction.

As we approached our camping ground, Floyd recognized an old acquaintance in the person of an English missionary, Mr. El Karey, long resident in Nablous, who followed us to our tents, and after a kindly welcome, offered to conduct us through the town, that is worth seeing, as it is next to Jerusalem in population, which it far surpasses in commercial activity. Nablous is one of the few places in the East that have been touched with the business life of the modern world. It seemed as if the rushing streams had communicated to the people a little of their own rapid movement. At least they have set the wheels of industry in motion. Besides the oil presses which receive the abundant yield of the olive orchards that we have seen all along our course, and turn it into oil, there are some twenty factories engaged in turning the oil into soap, which has become a large article of export to Jaffa and Beirut, and thence to all the ports of the Mediterranean. It was really refreshing, after passing through so many places that were more dead than alive, to come to one town that showed a sign of life in this sleepy old country.

But the chief interest of Nablous to a traveller is that it introduces him to the Samaritans. It is the only place in Palestine where there is a remnant of this ancient sect. In the town of Samaria itself there are no Samaritans ; all are at Nablous, and here they are very few, and fast fading away. A hundred and fifty souls is the whole remnant of the Samaritan people, counting men, women, and children ! Their fewness and feebleness are indicated by the pettiness of their synagogue—a small room, with bare whitewashed walls ; and yet it contains a manuscript of the Pentateuch (their Bible is limited to the Five Books of Moses) which they affirm is the oldest in the world, and regard as a priceless treasure. They claim that it was written by a great-grandson of Aaron ; certainly it is yellow enough to

have come out of the Ark.   They are such a " feeble folk,"
so few and so poor, that the high priest (a descendant of
the tribe of Levi) ekes out a living by showing travellers
the synagogue and the sacred scroll, and even offered to
sell us his photograph!   And yet such is the pride of an
ancient race, that this handful of Samaritans still cling to
the belief that they, and they only, are the true people of
God.   Three times a year they go up on Mount Gerizim,
and keep the festivals prescribed by the law of Moses,
while they celebrate the Passover by sacrifices—the only
people professing to worship Jehovah, who continue that
ancient rite.   Mount Gerizim is the only place in the
world where still ascends the smoke of sacrifice.   The
Passover is kept with the strictest observance of every
detail enjoined by Moses, with the hurried repast of bitter
herbs and unleavened bread, while they eat the Paschal
lamb with girdles about their loins, and staff in hand, as if
preparing for instant flight.   What is left is burned with
fire, in imitation of the ancient Israelites, who left only
ashes behind them, as they turned their backs on Egypt,
and took up their march through the desert.   The continued existence of such a fragment of people is an extraordinary spectacle, and is a subject for study.   I hardly
know anywhere of an instance of such tenacity of belief.
Here is a sect which was in existence in the time of Christ,
and probably hundreds of years before : for it is supposed
to date from the time of Nehemiah, when, not being permitted to share in the rebuilding of the Temple, they separated themselves from the Jews ; which has lived through
all the storms and persecutions of more than two thousand
years ; and which, it may be, will not die till it dies with
the race.   If there comes a time when there is a "last
man," it would be in keeping with the spirit of his race if
he were to go up on Mount Gerizim, and there build an

altar unto the Lord, and kindling a sacrifice, lie down to
die, that the flame of sacrifice and the flame of life might
expire together.

After our excursion, Mr. El Karey returned with us to
camp, and we kept him to dinner. With true American
inquisitiveness, I plied him with all sorts of questions
about the country and the people. He liked the town
very much. Indeed I believe he was born here: his name
is Eastern, though he was educated in England. He liked
the people, although they are very bigoted and fanatical
Moslems ; and when he first came in contact with them as
a missionary, the relation was not at all pleasant. But
acquaintance and intercourse had gradually softened their
animosity. In one respect he paid a high tribute to their
virtue. He said that anything like public prostitution,
the open and unblushing licentiousness which is the dis-
grace of European cities, was here absolutely unknown.
It will be said that the Moslem religion legalizes impurity
in another form, by its domestic customs. But whatever
the explanation, this seemed to me a very extraordinary
testimony to be borne to a Moslem people by a Christian
missionary.

He told us many things about the Bedaween. He had
made frequent excursions to the other side of the Jordan,
where there are some powerful tribes, which boast of their
tens of thousands of spears, and have more than once
defied the armies of the Sultan. Some years since the
Turkish government sent a large force against them, which
they defeated. The Bedaween are splendid horsemen, and
mustering in battle array, they rode down the Turkish
infantry with a rush that swept everything before them.
"Here is the place," said an old sheikh, riding over the
field with the missionary, and his eyes flashed as he said
"How we did give it to them!" The second time the

result was different. But, said the sheikh, unwilling to admit that they could be defeated in honorable battle, "it was not the Turks that beat us—*it was the children of the mules!*" It appeared that in the second battle, warned by their defeat, the Turks brought up a large force of artillery, using the same weapon with which Napoleon had destroyed the Mamelukes of Egypt. The cannon were drawn on the ground by mules, which being driven in front, looked at a distance like a procession of beasts of burden hauling a baggage train, until they parted to the right and left, and the batteries opened with shot and shell. This seemed to the Bedaween, accustomed to fight on horseback, an infernal device. In the confusion and uproar, no wonder that they imagined that the balls which cut through their ranks had somehow come from the mules, who seemed suddenly to have tongues of fire, and to hurl destruction out of their huge mouths. These "fiery darts" were "the children of the mules." It was, the first time that I knew that mules had children, but if they had, it seemed quite in character that such unnatural progeny should appear in flame and smoke.

These wild children of the desert could hardly be supposed to be very hopeful subjects of missionary labor, nor could he report much success. But at least they had received him kindly. He knew all their tribes, and went among them without fear ; and though they were a race of robbers, they did him no wrong. True, he took good care to carry nothing with him to tempt their cupidity. He went without scrip or purse, and always rode straight to the tent of the sheikh, and claimed his hospitality, and placed himself under his protection. Nor did they ever belie his confidence, or betray their guest. On the contrary, they had received him as if he had been one of their own tribe, and gave him the best they had, and he had

lain down in their tents, and slept in safety. They showed
him hospitality sometimes at great trouble to themselves.
One night he came to a tent, and was almost dying with
hunger, but saw no sign of preparation to satisfy his crav-
ing. He did not then know the reason, which was that
they had nothing to set before him. At last weary and
faint, he wrapped himself in his blanket and lay down,
hoping to forget the pangs of hunger in sleep. But presently he heard whisperings, and women left the tent, and
went out into the darkness. At last he dropped asleep,
and when he awoke it was broad day. He then learned
that the women had made a three hours journey on foot to
bring water from a spring to cook a breakfast for him, and
towards morning a sheep had been killed, and now was
set before him a feast which it had cost them all night to
prepare. No wonder he was touched by such kindness.
He said the Bedaween often paid him a visit when they
came to Nablous, and he always set food and drink before
them, and thus tried in some way to return the hospitality
shown him by the children of the desert.

These were pleasant things to talk about as we sat in
the gloaming under the ancient olive trees. At length he
rose to depart. " By the way," said the dragoman, "would
you be so kind as to stop at the headquarters of the officer
in command of the troops, and ask him to send us a guard
for the night?" "Of course." But really it seemed quite
unnecessary in a city so populous, and apparently so
thoroughly governed : for Nablous is one of the centres of
Turkish power in Palestine ; it has not only a governor,
but a garrison in command of an officer of high rank, who
had under him, it was said, a thousand men. We saw
their barracks as we rode up the valley. It was not an
unpleasant sight in this lawless country. I confess it gave
us a sense of security to feel that we had come at last

within the range of guns. It seemed as if such a military force were enough to hold in check any propensities of an ill-disposed population, if such there were, and that we needed no special guard. However, just for the dignity of the thing, we submitted to this military protection, and perhaps were a little lifted up in mind when four soldiers filed into camp, and took their places, one before each tent. What a sense of greatness it gives to the most insignificant traveller to see a soldier standing guard before his door! With such a protector, I lay down to sleep, feeling as did another in fancied security, when

> "At midnight, in his guarded tent,
> The Turk was dreaming of the hour."

Such were my dreams, when bang! went a gun, and there was a sound of feet scurrying to and fro. But even that excited no alarm, for though it betokened danger, it showed that the guardians of our safety were awake and vigilant; so like the dreaming Turk, I turned and went to sleep again. But as the dawn of day crept slowly on, for it was raining, and the morning was dark and lowery, the drago-man appeared at the door of the tent, with a troubled face, to ask "if we had been robbed." "Robbed? No. Why do you ask?" "Because your neighbors in the next tent *have been*." So much for our military protectors! The next tent was occupied by Mr. and Mrs. Winter, the English gentleman and his wife, who had taken extraordinary precautions to insure the safety of their valuables, which were locked in a travelling-bag that was always kept with them, and when they retired to their tent, was fastened to the tent-pole! But in the night some one had cut through the canvas of the tent, and creeping softly between the two iron bedsteads, whose occupants were sleeping, cut the fastening and dragged off the precious bag, which was found not a hundred yards from the tent, rifled of its con-

tents, including a sandal-wood box, which contained a
number of souvenirs picked up on the Continent, among
them a pair of bracelets that had cost a hundred and fifty
pounds! Here was a sensation which brought us all to
our feet and out of our tents. Our first thought was,
What inexcusable negligence on the part of our guards!
until a little further reflection led us to think that perhaps the guards were themselves the robbers! This idea
took such strong hold of us that as we turned to look at
them, their blank faces seemed a silent confession of
guilt, and we had them at once seized by our muleteers,
and marched off to the office of the military command-
ant, to receive instant punishment for their crime. Mr.
Winter and the dragoman went along to witness their
condemnation. Whoever has been in an Eastern court,
knows that it is a place where justice is rendered, if rendered at all, "without mercy." The Colonel was at his
headquarters, and as soon as he heard the story, ordered
the soldiers into his presence, and accused them directly
of the crime, bursting out upon them in a rage and fury
that were really appalling. They were thieves, robbers,
wretches of the blackest dye. "He knew their guilt ; they
could not deceive him." If they did not at once return
the stolen goods, he would have them beaten within an
inch of their lives. This violence of language was accompanied with such violence of manner, that those who heard
him almost looked to see the wretched creatures thrown
on the ground and bastinadoed on the spot. Nor would
bastinadoing be sufficient ; he would "tear out their eyes
from their sockets," and "cut their tongues from their
throats"! Even then his wrath would not be appeased :
he would have their wives and children made beggars, or
sold as slaves! Those who listened, thought that the
majesty of justice had never appeared in a form so awful ;

that "Turkish justice" at least was more than a name ; that it was a fearful reality, since it was now to be vindicated before their eyes by a retribution so swift and terrible.

An hour passed, and a change came over the spirit of our dream. Scarcely had Floyd returned to the camp before we saw through the trees some important personage approaching, and soon appeared the officer in command himself, with half a dozen attendants, and with our guards, who were marched on the ground to be confronted with their accusers. They protested their innocence, though they contradicted themselves in a way to leave little doubt of their guilt. The officer dismounted with a somewhat haughty air, and was conducted to a tent, where, being first supplied with coffee and cigarettes, he took his seat of state, and summoning his secretary to take our " depositions," desired to make further injury into the " alleged " robbery suffered by members of our party. It had suddenly dawned upon him that he had been too hasty in admitting that we had been robbed by his own men. Was it to be supposed that " soldiers " would be thieves ; that the guardians of the law would be the breakers of the law ? To confess this would be an imputation on their military honor, which he could not admit without the strongest proof. How did we know that our own muleteers were not the thieves ? He seemed now fully convinced that our English friends had been robbed by the retainers of our own party, *if indeed they had been robbed at all*, for the more he thought about it, the more it seemed to his judicial mind as if the whole story were, to use a slang phrase, " a put up job." This was made probable to him by the large amount of the loss. " How much did you say," he asked of Mr. Winter, " you had lost ? " " A hundred and fifty pounds." " That is a great deal," he answered, " as much

as a merchant would carry who was travelling with goods
to sell. A hundred and fifty pounds!" he repeated,
adding with a sneer, "Why do you not make it a thousand?" evidently thinking one story as probable as the
other. So saying, he mounted his horse, followed by his
secretary and other attendants, and rode away.

We were now placed in an awkward position. Not
only had members of our party been robbed, but they were
under suspicion of being privy to a pretended crime of
which they had accused others, to extort money from the
Turkish government.

To add to the cheerfulness of the situation, it had been
raining all night, and promised to rain all day. We could
not put a foot out of the tents without stepping in mud.
Indeed the rain invaded our tents, and we were almost
afloat. We wrapped ourselves in waterproofs, and put
rubbers on our feet, and thus muffled up, gathered under
the olive trees where but a few hours ago we had sat in
the twilight, and talked of the hospitality and other virtues
of the descendants of Ishmael. It was a dismal company.
The dragoman looked at me, and I looked at my fellow-
travellers, and they looked at the horses, whose manes and
tails were limp and dripping, and the horses looked at
the mules ; and all, man and beast, seemed bound together
in one companionship of misery. We were disgusted, not
only at the robbery, but at our impotence to punish it. I
will not say that we "cursed our fate," for that would have
been wicked ; but I am afraid some of my countrymen,
who are not very choice in their language, would have
described the exhibition of that morning as a specimen of
"pure cussedness." If we could have followed our impulse, I believe we should at that moment have struck our
tents, and mounted our horses, and turned our backs on
Nablous, preferring to face the storm rather than to be

thus enraged and defied. But even if we did not care for
the fury of the elements, we were reluctant to execute a
manœuvre which would look like a retreat in face of the
enemy. So we determined heroically to stay and see it out.

After another hour of reflection, we plucked up courage and resolved to make one more attempt. This time
we would beard the lion in his den—we would go to the
Governor himself. And that we might impress him with
a sense of our importance, we would go in a body. So
gathering up our garments, as if we would shake off the
dust, or rather the mud, from our feet, we marched
through the streets to the Serai, the official residence, and
demanded an audience. We were admitted into the court,
and shown up a stone staircase into an ante-room (which
had a look of extreme dilapidation) to wait the pleasure of
his highness. Impatient as we were, it was reviving to
have the attendant who went to seek his master return
after a few minutes' absence, and inform us that he was
asleep, and could not be disturbed, but that he would
awake some time in the forenoon, and after his breakfast,
would perhaps see us, unless he had more important matters or personages to claim his attention! Again we
looked in each other's faces, and behold, they were very
blank. If there be any thing in the world that will take
one's sense of dignity, or of his own consequence, out of
him, it is to be dancing attendance in the ante-room of an
Eastern official, with whom time is of no consequence. It
*was* rather tedious. If we had had any " news " to feed
upon, even the smallest bit of gossip to nibble at, it
would have stayed our utter vacuity of mind. But no, we
had nothing to talk about or think about except our own
wretched selves, and we were in that disgusted state in
which a man holds himself in contempt, thinking "You
are a pretty fool to get into such a scrape." To relieve the

monotony we would now and then walk to the window and look out, but could see nothing but rain, rain, rain. This might not have been quite so tiresome if we could have seen any living thing. Washington Irving has written a very pleasant sketch of " a rainy day " which he passed in a country inn. But he could look into a barnyard, with its busy, bustling brood. If we could have seen a rooster, and heard him crow, or a hen and chickens, that would have been quite sufficient to set us off into a talk about domestic fowls. But there was no sign of bird or beast : the rain fell into a stone-paved court, hard and cruel as our fate. So after staring at the stones, we came back from the window and sat down again, all in a row, like convicts in the box, waiting for sentence. In this interesting occupation we passed two mortal hours, when there was a stir without, and the Governor in a fez cap mounted the stairs and entered the room, and making us a gracious salaam, took his seat on the divan. He was not quite the ideal of a Turkish pacha, who ought always to be fat : for he was a little man, with hardly flesh enough on his bones to support so much dignity. The only touch of Oriental magnificence about him was the heavy rings worn on his dainty fingers. As he sat on the edge of the divan, his feet dangled to the floor, which they hardly touched, and he appeared to be sitting uncomfortably, until suddenly he drew up his legs, which, when coiled under him like a cushion, furnished a sufficient base for the slender superstructure. Thus supported, his vertebral column stood up more erect, and swayed hither and thither like a serpent, as he bowed to our petition and complaint. I have no doubt he wished us all in Jericho. However, he was civil, and asked many questions, and made us soft speeches, the full value of which we soon understood. After a somewhat long interview, in which he professed great sympathy for our loss, and made many promises, he bowed us out just as wise as we were before, and fully convinced that our plain, straightforward ways, unless backed by force, were no match for Oriental cunning and duplicity.

When we came out into the street, it was still pouring, and as it was dismal to go back to our tents to pass the rest of the day, and another night, perhaps to be robbed again, we accepted the invitation of the missionary to transfer our quarters to his house, where, though we were packed pretty closely, and though, when night came, some of us had to sleep on the floor, we had at least a roof over our heads, and a barred door between us and any robbers who might be prowling about. We were wet and shivering, but we sat round the charcoal-burner till we got thoroughly warmed—a sensation which restored a little the equanimity of our minds.

We did not go out again that day. We had had enough of Nablous, and were in no mood to make any further explorations of this sacred city. Though we had camped at the foot of Mount Gerizim, we did not climb to the top where sacrifices had been offered for more than two thousand years. Indeed of the two I think we should have felt more inclined to go up on Mount Ebal, and read all the curses of the law over a place which had proved to us—not a holy mount, but a den of thieves.

But we would not pronounce a malediction on a place where we had found at last a shelter. Here we were warmed and fed, and in the returning sense of comfort, we could listen with complacence to the rain which still poured heavily in the streets. There is a sweet sense of security in the sound of pattering rain, not when it falls on soaking tents, but on a firm and tight roof. Thus we passed the rest of the day in the quiet and comfort of the missionary's home.

To make an end of this story of robbery, I will antici-
pate a little. The next morning, before leaving Nablous,
Mr. Winter, with the dragoman, paid a second visit to the
Governor, and found him in a gracious mood. He did
not, like the Colonel, question the truth of their tale, but
promised the fullest reparation. The stolen property
should be restored to the very last mite. Not only the
costly jewelry, but every trifle to the last brass pin. It
might take several days, but when we reached Nazareth,
or at farthest Damascus or Beirut, the whole missing
property should be placed in the hands of the owner,
untouched. These assurances were given, if not with the
formality of an oath, yet with all the sacred sanction of
honor and truth. He followed our friends to the door,
repeating these assurances, so that the very last words
they heard were what so many other travellers in the East
have to hear—lying Turkish promises! But these false
words accomplished their purpose, of raising a flutter of
hope in the breasts of our robbed companions. For a
time they felt even a little return of confidence, and were
buoyed up as we resumed our march by seeing their
treasures in the distance, which they continued to see very
much in the distance all the way through Palestine. At
each stage of our journey the pledge was freshly recalled
to be freshly disappointed. At last, when we sailed from
Beirut for Constantinople, we left our English friends at
the hotel still waiting for Turkish justice! If they were
determined not to depart till they had recovered what
they had lost, I fear they are waiting there still. Such
was our day in Nablous—a day that was certainly not all
sunshine. May we never see its like again!

# CHAPTER IX.

## TO SAMARIA AND JENIN—FALLING AGAIN AMONG THIEVES.

Half the pleasure of life is in contrast, in change from one scene to another. "The clear shining after rain" is beautiful *because* of the rain, which has cleansed and purified the atmosphere, and made the air so sweet and the sky so blue. But for "the rain" which has gone before, we might not appreciate "the clear shining" which follows after. So in our human experience there is a peculiar zest given to that which is pleasant, by the fact that it comes after that which is dismal and forlorn. Such a change we experienced the next morning. When the day broke, "the rain was over and gone," and the sun rose without a cloud. A little after seven we mounted our horses before the missionary's door, and began to file through the streets of Nablous, followed by the train of mules carrying our tents. Everything wore a new aspect. The city had been washed clean by the rains of the preceding day, and the olive orchards on the hillsides were fresh and green. As the sun touched the tops of the twin mountains between which the valley lies, we could not find it in our hearts to pronounce a malediction even upon Ebal, when it answered so beamingly to the first flush of day. As we rode down the valley, the streams by the roadside, swollen by the rains, seemed to be running a race, bubbling and boiling over in their fulness of joy. These streams unite below the town, and flow through the Plain of Sharon to the Mediterranean. We knew that the sea was not many miles away, for a delicious sea-breeze came up from the west, and blew in our faces, filling our lungs with such bracing air that we felt a constant impulse to shout and sing. Every living thing seemed to have caught the inspiration : the time of the singing of birds had come, and the flowers appeared on the earth. The innumerable multitudes of wild flowers is one of the beauties of Palestine, and never were they more abundant or of more exquisite variety, than that morning as we rode through the hills and valleys of ancient Samaria. This is the heart of Palestine, its central region, and is at once the most beautiful in natural scenery, and the most richly cultivated. It is indeed a land of corn and wine, of vineyards and oliveyards, of the fig-tree and the pomegranate, and of brooks that run among the hills. Through landscapes so rich and varied we rode for a couple of hours, when we saw in the distance a hill standing alone—an island in a sea of verdure—its sides terraced and blooming with the olive and the vine, like those sunny slopes along the Corniche road, in France and Italy, which open their breasts to be warmed by the Southern sun. Below it and around it stretched a wide plain, beyond which rose the encircling hills ; so that the central height, standing solitary, was like a throne set in the midst of a vast amphitheatre.

On this noble eminence stood the ancient city of Samaria—a city whose origin dates from nine hundred years before Christ, when Omri, King of Israel, bought the

hill for two talents of silver, and built a city upon it, which
he called after the name of Shemer, the owner of the hill,
Samaria. Here a hundred years later we find a splendid
capital, in which Ahab, ruled by a pagan wife, built the
temple of Baal and his palace of ivory, and where Jezebel
(the Lady Macbeth of a king perhaps more weak than
wicked) led him to play the tyrant over his unhappy people. That the city must have had great resources, appears
from the fact that it withstood a three years' siege from
the army of the Syrians, which came down from the north,
and beleaguered the place till the inhabitants were ready
to die with famine, and even began to devour each other,
when it was delivered by a Divine interposition, in accordance with the prediction of Elisha. We are now in the
country of Elijah and Elisha, whose prophet forms are con-
tinually appearing and disappearing and reappearing in
the history of the Kings of Israel.

The beauty of the position of Samaria attracted the
eyes of the Roman conquerors, who made it the capital of Central Palestine. Here Herod the Great, who
had a passion for splendid architecture, and was always
building palaces, erected that long colonnade the remains
of which still attest its ancient magnificence. We rode up
the hill, and leaving our horses in charge of the muleteers, set out on a walk around the brow of the plateau,
tracing this colonnade. It is over half a mile long, and
must have numbered hundreds of columns. Sixty are still
standing, after nineteen centuries. When first erected,
this long line of marble columns, standing on the crest of a
hill, from which it could be seen to a great distance over
the country, must have seemed like a royal crown for the
monarch's brow. It was standing in the time of Christ,
and as He often passed through Samaria on his way from
Nazareth to Jerusalem, he must have seen it in all its

splendor. But not once does he make allusion to it ; so much less in his eye were princes and palaces than humbler beings in their obscure abodes ; so much less was the whiteness of marble columns than the purity of a human soul.

Of course Samaria, like other towns in Palestine, is but the shadow of its former self—a wretched village taking the place of the former capital. The city is gone, but the beauty of the country remains. It came upon us anew as we passed round the hill, and came out on the northern slope, and looked down on the terraced hillsides, and the wide expanse below, over which the light and shadow were playing. Descending into the plain, we rode through its rich fields, and then over the hills and through the fertile vales. A little to one side was Dothan, where Joseph's brethren cast him into a pit, and afterwards drew him out to sell him to the Midianites, who carried him down to Egypt, and where Elisha saw the mountains round about filled with horses and chariots of fire! These were great memories, which might well arrest the travel-ler ; but we could not turn aside even for these, for it had again set in to rain. This matter of rain is an element that must never be left out of calculation. The month of April is considered the best for Palestine, because it is free from rain ; at least it is supposed to be. The early rains come, not in the Spring, but in the Autumn, when the husbandmen plow and sow. The latter rains come in the Spring, and ripen the harvest. These are supposed to end in March, so that properly there *ought* not to be any rain in April. But this year the seasons are out of joint. Thus far our two drawbacks to the pleasure of travel in Palestine have been rains and thieves. There has been a flood of rains and an epidemic of thieves. To-day the rain began soon after noon, and kept on pour-

ing harder and harder. As we climbed over the hills, with
the wind driving in our faces, we found it difficult to make
head against the combined wind and rain. The bravery of
my military carriage disappeared. With all my desire to
keep a heroic attitude, I had to confess that a traveller,
with garments bedraggled and bespattered, trying (with
poor success) to keep an umbrella over his head, is not
quite like a mailed and helmeted Crusader. Of course our
first impulse would have been to stop and go into camp;
but the baggage mules had gone forward with the tents,
and we must keep on, for we had no shelter. So we made
the best of it, and struggled on through the storm, thank-
ful at last, though drenched and weary, to reach a place of
rest. We had been in the saddle ten hours.

We found our tents pitched at Jenin, on the edge of the
great Plain of Esdraelon. It is a town of several thousand
inhabitants, with a mosque, and has rather a pretty look,
embowered in trees, in which, among the olive orchards,
rise a few stately palms that speak of a sunnier clime. We
camped outside of the town, but near enough to hear the
muezzin, as from the top of the minaret he called the faithful to prayer. This call to prayer is always pleasant to hear
at the close of day, as it seems to say that we have reached a
place sacred to devotion, and therefore the abode of quiet-
ness and peace. Our dragoman, no doubt, was sensible to
all these soothing associations; but warned by our experience at Nablous, and not placing unbounded confidence in
Moslem prayers or Moslem guards, he determined not to
trust to any outside defenders, but to keep watch himself.
The task was made more difficult by the dark nights. Our
moonlight nights had left us in Jerusalem, so that now we
had only starlight, and in these frequent rains not even
that; so that the nights were "pitch dark," and dark
nights seem made for dark deeds. However, the drago-

man did the best he could. He had Chinese lanterns hung in front and rear of every tent, and two fires burning on the opposite sides of the camp, with a man at each fire, and another all the time moving about. He himself was to snatch a little sleep in the early watches, but to be called at midnight.

With such protection we "turned in" for the night, and fell asleep. It was a little past midnight when suddenly my tent door opened, and a tall form appeared. I awoke and sat up, and supposing it to be the dragoman, who was to go on watch at midnight, I called him by name, but received no answer. Then it flashed upon me that I was honored with the visit of a "stranger," and springing from the bed I seized Weeden and shook him to awaken him. In a moment Floyd came rushing to the tent. "Strike a light!" was his first word. In an instant we had a candle and made a search, but found nothing, and I began to think it was a false alarm, a dream, or some wild fancy of the night. But there was the tent door open, which Floyd had fastened securely two or three hours before. It was all a mystery, but I might still have thought it an illusion but for what followed. We had shut the door again and put out the light, and were resting quietly, though but half asleep, when a little after two we heard a pistol shot, followed by a rush, and then crack, crack, crack, half a dozen shots in succession, as fast as one could pull a trigger. Presently the dragoman appeared, and the story was soon told. The Chinese lanterns had been blown out by the wind, and the rain had extinguished the fires, so that the camp was left in darkness. Floyd was groping about when he saw very faintly the figure of a man near the tent of the Winters. Thinking it was one of the muleteers who were at that hour on watch, he called "Joseph," and "Moses," but receiving no reply, he called to the shadow "Who are you?" when the figure dropped instantly in the grass. Then he cried to the men, "Here's a thief, come and catch him," at which the man sprang up and ran, with a bullet after him to quicken his steps, and the same moment two others sprang up and joined in his flight. Floyd snapped his pistol again, but it would not go off. It took him a moment to fumble in his pocket for another and larger revolver, which did *not* miss fire. His blood was up, and he let fly shot after shot. However, the thieves made good time, and were soon lost in the darkness. The whole affair occupied but a few moments, but it left us in a state of great excitement. All the men were up, and for them there was no more sleep till morning. Chinese lanterns were lighted again at every tent, both in front and rear. As the whole camp was now on guard, we, who were "only passengers," felt that we were safer than ever before, and lying down for the third time, slept as we could till morning.

I am sorry to have so much to say about thieves, but the fault is not in me, but in the thieves. If they had not been there, I should not have had to speak about them. They have taken me a little off my guard. I thought when we left the desert, that we had entered the bounds of civilization. After our experience with the Bedaween, I hoped we were done with perils of robbers. But the worst was to come after we left Jerusalem. I do not wish to make too much of these incidents, nor to exaggerate them into real "perils." There has been no tragedy. Only I have had a little taste of what other travellers have had in fuller measure. It is the usage of the country, to which we must all submit. "A certain man went down to Jericho, and fell among thieves." He has had many successors, and they do not all find a good Samaritan. For

this travellers should be prepared. So much is it a matter
of course, that a tour in the Holy Land is hardly complete without a robbery.

Comparing our experience with others, we do not find
that we have fared worse than they. This year has been a
harvest time for thieves, and few have escaped. An American gentleman whom we met in Jerusalem—Mr. Chapin
of Providence—left the day before us. We met him again
in Nazareth, when he told us his experience. On the
second night he camped at Howara, an hour and a half
before reaching Nablous, and applied to the sheikh of the
village for a guard, who sent three men. In the night
a man entered his tent, and carried off his wife's car-
pet-bag; but finding little in it, came again, and carried
off his portmanteau. By this time his suspicions were
excited, and he gave the alarm, which brought the dragoman to his tent, who, understanding the ways of the
country, put his pistol to the head of the chief man of the
guard, and told him to bring back the portmanteau. In a
few minutes he brought it. It was found outside the tent,
where it had been opened. The guards of course protested their innocence, but the dragoman was not deceived
by them; but sure that they were the thieves, called his
muleteers, and ordered them to seize the sheikh and bind
him. No quicker said than done. Instantly they threw
him on the ground, and lashed his hands behind his back.
In this condition the dragoman tied him with a strong
rope to his horse's head, and literally drove him before
him. The others were taken in hand by the muleteers,
and thus all were marched to Nablous, where they were
recognized as old offenders, and lodged in prison.

This constant exposure to the danger of being robbed,
is the great drawback to the pleasure of travel in Palestine.
Robbery is the curse of the country, as brigandage has

been for generations the curse of Sicily. How it is to be
extirpated is a difficult problem. The fault is not merely
in the people; it is in this wretched Turkish government,
which is as weak as it is corrupt, and which, by its total
failure to encourage honest industry, almost compels the
miserable people to steal in order to live. It discourages
honesty, and offers a premium to crime. Such a deep-
seated disease can only be cured by heroic surgery. I
hear a great deal said about this country's being "evan-
gelized"; but it needs first to be governed—to be ruled
justly and firmly. Moral influences, when they can have a
chance to operate, will bring other blessings in their train.
But for the present we must rely upon the strong arm.
The country must be governed with an iron hand.

# CHAPTER X.

A RIDE OVER THE PLAIN OF ESDRAELON.

/ Promptly at the hour of sunrise the muezzin climbed the minaret of the mosque of Jenin, and called the faithful to prayer ; but his wailing, melancholy cry did not awaken the same pensive musing as when we heard it at the hour of sunset. After a night of alarms, of men running and shots firing, with a robber at the door of my tent, I was not in a mood to indulge in the luxury of sentimental devotion. We felt no desire to "dwell in the tents" of Jenin any longer, but were quite ready to depart.

The morning, however, was not one for rapid movement. The dark and dismal night still lowered over the opening day. The clouds hung low upon the hills, and fast fell the drops which the wind blew angrily in our faces. Prudent travellers would perhaps have lingered awhile before leaving camp. But it was the last day of the week, and we were bent on spending Sunday in Nazareth ; and after our experience of the night, if it had "rained pitch-forks" we should have wished to move on. So girding up our loins, and muffling up our breasts, we mounted our horses, and set our faces to the storm. /

The result proved the wisdom of our course. When a

man or a party is "in the dumps," a solemn, silent mood
that may sour into sullenness, there is nothing like the
"movement cure." In travelling, as in other things that
demand instant action, the American rule is a good one
that "the only way to do a thing is to do it," and not
stand thinking about it till the time for action is past.
However formidable the attempt may appear, it is probable that the reality will not prove so serious as the
anticipation. Once in the saddle, the exercise gave us a
sensation of life; the blood began to tingle in our veins,
and to set our dull thoughts in motion. Instead of drawing thick wraps over our stooping shoulders, we straight-
ened up and began to look about and to study the
geography of the country. We found that we had come
into a new part of Palestine; that we had left the hills
and come down into the plains, a change which was
grateful to the eye, as we had been riding for days over
a very rugged country. We were now in the great Plain
of Esdraelon, so famous in Jewish history—a plain which
is not monotonous like our Western prairies, because it is
set in an amphitheatre of hills. Central in position, it
makes a break between the Hill Country of the South and
the Mountain Country of the North, and thus at once
separates and unites the two great divisions of Palestine.
The beauty of this Plain is not only in its fertility, which
in this month of April makes it one broad expanse of green,
but in its bordering of hills—a feature which reminded me
of the Parks of Colorado, although the resemblance extends
only to this, that in each case there is a broad plain lying
in the lap of hills which enfold it, and seem to stand guard
around it. As to magnitude, there is no comparison: for
the whole of Palestine is but a representation in miniature
of the central State of our continent, traversed by the great
chain of the Rocky Mountains. Here both mountain and

plain are on a very reduced scale. Compared with the Middle Park or the South Park of Colorado, the Plain of Esdraelon is of very moderate dimensions, while the mountains around it are but foot-hills beside the American Alps.

But whatever this Plain may want in natural grandeur, it more than makes up by historical associations. Its horizon is like that of the Roman Campagna, where every summit of the Sabine and the Alban Hills has its legend and story. Those hills on the South, which we are leaving behind, were once held by the powerful tribe of Manasseh, which played such a heroic part in the Jewish wars ; that long ridge on the West, stretching to the Mediterranean Sea, is Mount Carmel, the retreat of the Prophets Elijah and Elisha ; on the East, standing apart, are the heights of Mount Gilboa and Mount Tabor ; while in front of us to the North, rise the Hills of Galilee.

The natural divisions of the country determined its political divisions. In ancient times, when communication was slow and difficult, some natural feature of a country— a mountain or plain or river—was the barrier interposed by nature, which separated one kingdom, or province, from another. Thus the Province of Samaria ended with the hills, and in descending to the plain, we enter another province which figures far more conspicuously in the New Testament history—that of Galilee. /

Riding over the plain, a couple of hours brought us to a hill, on which is perched a wretched village, but which was once a habitation of princes ; for this is JEZREEL, where Ahab, when he had his capital in Samaria, had his country palace, his Versailles, which was the scene of many a revel and many a tragedy. Here was Naboth's vineyard, of which Jezebel, more resolute than her cowardly husband Ahab, who did not dare to strike, stirred him up to get

possession by plotting the murder of its owner—a crime to
be avenged on herself, for here infuriated men threw the
wicked queen out of the palace window, and in Naboth's
vineyard the dogs licked up her blood! Of such tragic
tales, how much of ancient history is made up, and of
modern history also; for human nature does not change
with the progress of civilization, and human selfishness,
however veiled by forms, is still the same. Boast as we
may of "new men, new times," we find in every age the
same old world, "the same old crimes."∕

But we are in the neighborhood of a tragedy greater
and more mournful than the death of Ahab and Jezebel,
for the hill of Jezreel is at the western extremity of Mount
Gilboa, on which the Israelites were defeated by the Phil-
istines—a national calamity, which threatened the ruin of
the Hebrew State, but the interest of which to after generations has been more of a personal character, since on
that field perished Saul and Jonathan, whose unhappy fate
was mourned by David in one of the most beautiful strains
of elegiac poetry that ever touched the heart of the world.
Looking up to that elevated plateau, where the battle
raged and "the mighty" fell, the traveller cannot help
recalling the lamentation, which was the more surprising
because the life of him who made it had been sought by
him over whom he lamented. Yet as a loyal Hebrew,
David could not but mourn the defeat of his people and
the death of their king. Hence this outburst of patriotic
grief: "The beauty of Israel is slain upon thy high places;
how are the mighty fallen! Ye mountains of Gilboa, let
there be no dew, neither let there be rain upon you [a
malediction which seems to be fulfilled in its rocky desola-
tion], for there the shield of the mighty was vilely cast
away." But the keenest sorrow of the minstrel is for the
death of his friend : "I am distressed for thee, my brother

Jonathan : very pleasant hast thou been unto me : thy love to me was wonderful, passing the love of women." Yet with what grace does he include both in this : " Saul and Jonathan were lovely and pleasant in their lives, and in their death they were not divided."

These sad dirges are relieved by a more jubilant strain as we ride over the hill of Jezreel, and on the further slope come upon the fountain of Gideon, the heroic leader, who with his little band of three hundred—just as many as the Greeks had at Thermopylæ—stole in the darkness of night upon the enemy scattered far and wide upon the plains, and by the suddenness and vigor of the attack, created a panic in the camp of the Amalekites, which sent them down the valley of Jezreel in so hurried flight, that they stayed not till they had passed over the fords of the dividing river and sought safety in their own country on the other side of the Jordan. /

Leaving Jezreel with its heroic and its bloody memories, another hour's ride brings us to a spot with more tender associations, where in place of the haughty Jezebel, our interest gathers round a poor woman and her dead child, for this is Shunem, the scene of the raising of the Shunemite's son. On this hill once stood a village in which Elisha, coming from Carmel, often found a home in the house of a good woman, who had prepared him a prophet's chamber and showed him hospitality, a kindness which was to return to her when in the hour of her despair she sought him among the rocks of his mountain retreat. Hither he came at her call to give comfort to the mourner by giving life to the dead. What a pathos there is in these old Bible stories! The place is not far removed from that of a second resurrection, for it is but an hour's ride from Shunem to Nain, where our Lord met the funeral procession passing from the gates.

There is nothing in all the Gospels—not even the raising of Lazarus, which is more tender than that which is told in these few words : "Behold a dead man carried out—the only son of his mother and she was a widow! And when the Lord saw her, he had compassion on her and said unto her, Weep not. And he came and touched the bier : and they that bare him stood still. And he said, Young man, I say unto thee, Arise. And he that was dead sat up and began to speak. And he delivered him to his mother."/

In the present village of Shunem there is nothing sacred but a memory. Like the greater number of villages in Palestine, it is only a collection of mud hovels. We rode through it stared at by all the men, women and children, gathered at the doors, and barked at by all the dogs, which took good care to keep at a safe distance, as they were mounted on the roofs, from which they yelped defiance at the stranger. The people flocked after us to the further side of the village, where we halted, and turning aside from the bridle path through a cactus hedge, to a quiet spot, we hitched our horses to the trees, and spreading ourselves on a slope under the shade of a clump of fig trees, proceeded to discuss our luncheon, at which a large proportion of the population "assisted." It was a hungry looking crowd. Indeed it may be said that these people are always hungry : they always have a famished look. I have a guilty feeling as we enjoy our plentiful repasts at seeing poor children sit round with hungry eyes, as if they did not know what it was to have a full meal, and who snap at anything that we cast away, licking clean every tin box that has been packed with sardines, and gnawing on every chicken bone. I hardly wonder that they grow up a generation of thieves, when they see travellers pass by, well clothed and well fed, while they are both hungry and naked. The head man of the village has not a good reputation. Floyd drew his picture for us (it was well the sheikh did not understand English) while we now and then gave a side glance at him, noticing his ill-favored countenance. We imagined him to be debating in his mind whether he should rob us, or be content with levying toll, or begging a large backsheesh. Happily he chose the latter, perhaps thinking discretion the better part of valor, but he and his people literally " ate us up " with their eyes, and as we mounted for our journey, stood watching us till the last horse had disappeared in the distance. /

As we descended once more upon the broad spaces of Esdraelon, with a fair field before us, it seemed as if now were a good time for that " gentle knight," whom we have been so long expecting, to " come pricking o'er the plain "; but any equestrian performances on our part were checked by the state of the soil under our horses' feet : for the "latter rains " had done their work so effectually that the Plain of Esdraelon was what Robert Hall declared Gill's Body of Divinity to be—" a continent of mud." With such impediments to our rapid movement, we, who were of a sober turn of mind, moved slowly. But Floyd and my tent-mate, Weeden, who were both well mounted and fond of a chase, seized the slightest occasion to try the mettle of their horses. Just now the dragoman points to a hamlet on a hillside, an hour's ride away, as Endor, where Saul went to consult the Witch of Endor on the night before his last battle ; and instantly they bound away, as if the Witch of Endor had dashed at their horses' heels, which fly at her touch like Tam O'Shanter's mare. /

But we who jog along more quietly, have plenty of occupation for our thoughts in the historical recollections which rise from the ground on every part of this cele-brated plain. It has been the battle-field not only of

Palestine, but of all the East. The physical character of the country has determined its military history—its wars, battles, and sieges. When the Israelites crossed the Jordan, they advanced against the hills, and their earlier battles were fought with the mountain tribes which held the passes of Benjamin. But the Plain of Esdraelon—like that of Philistia—was formed for great armies, and has been marched over by kings and conquerors, coming from Assyria and Babylon on the East, and Egypt on the South, who have met in this great plain as their field of battle. Such an open space admitted of a style of warfare not possible among the mountains. When the Israelites, who had been victorious over the hill-tribes, came to the "low country," they shrank with terror from a new enemy with new weapons of war, and murmured bitterly that the Canaanites, who "dwelt in the land of the valley," had chariots of iron. But even these were not invincible by courage, for here Barak, inspired by the song of Deborah, rushed from the hills and swept away the nine hundred iron chariots of Sisera. As we ride along this plain, now so still and quiet, we recall the terrible scenes it has witnessed, and seem to hear the tread of the mighty hosts that have swept over it. This way passed the army of Sennacherib :

> The Assyrian came down like the wolf on the fold,
> His cohorts were gleaming in purple and gold,
> And the sheen of their spears was like stars on the sea,
> When the blue wave rolls nightly on deep Galilee.

The Assyrian has been followed by the Roman, the Crusader, and the Turk. Even the sacred height of Mount Tabor has given name to a battle which was fought, not upon it, but in sight of it, and on this plain, by Napoleon, when, marching from Egypt by way of Jaffa, (where he left a name still held in horror by his inhuman massacre of prisoners,) he was attempting the conquest of Syria, from which he could march on Constantinople, and thus "enter Europe by the back door." His daring dream of conquest was stopped but a few miles from this by the stubborn resistance of a few English troops that held the fortress of Acre.

Here soldiers of all nations have plunged their swords in each others' breasts, and falling face to face, have cursed each other in all the languages of men. The soil is rich and heavy with the blood of countless armies. With these clouds of war hanging over it, it is not strange that in the Apocalypse, the last great conflict of the world, which is to precede the reign of universal peace, is pictured as the battle of Armageddon—that is, of Megiddo, the ancient name of the Plain of Esdraelon. /

From these scenes of battle and blood, we turn to a spot associated with memories of the Prince of Peace. On the northeastern edge of the plain stands Mount Tabor, long supposed to be the mount of the Transfiguration. The tradition is now generally discredited, and the scene of that wonderful apparition is placed on Mount Hermon overlooking Banias, the ancient Cæsarea-Philippi. One cannot but regret the effect of modern research, when it disturbs a belief so long accepted, and so in accord with the fitness of the place itself. Tabor differs wholly from the other mountain of the plain, Gilboa, whose summit is bare and bleak, while Tabor is wooded and green, as if made to be pressed by angels' feet. Of majestic height, its lofty dome rising to an altitude that lifts it quite above the damps and mists of the plain into a purer atmosphere, it stands midway between earth and heaven, as if to invite visitants from the other world to an interview, from which, unseen by mortal eyes, they might return to their heavenly home. /

But even Tabor fades in interest as it fades in sight, as

the westering sun strikes on the Hills of Galilee, now rising before us. They do not rise abruptly, but by a gradual
ascent, so that we wind hither and thither as we climb
slowly upward, till at length we see in the distance a village nestled among the hills, in a valley so narrow as to be
almost a glen. That little mountain town is Nazareth! The
first glimpse hushed us, as did the first sight of Jerusalem,
for we were coming upon holy ground. Before us was one
of the places of pilgrimage that we most desired to see in
all Palestine ; as one of the few in a land under Moslem
rule which is sacred only to the memory of our Lord.
Jesus was born in Bethlehem, and died in Jerusalem, but
the greater part of his life was spent in Nazareth. As we
climbed up the steep approach, but one thought was present
to us—how often the Holy Child had rambled over these
hills. Full of such musings, we rode through the town to
the northwestern side, where we pitched our tents on a
rising ground, from which we looked down into the valley.
It was Saturday evening! If Burns wrote so touchingly
of the Cotter's Saturday night in Scotland, what might a
traveller, if he were only inspired with a little of the genius
of Burns, write of the evening shades, the gathering
twilight, which fell upon him on a Saturday evening in
Nazareth ?

# CHAPTER XI.

## NAZARETH—RENAN'S LIFE OF JESUS—CAN THAT LIFE BE EXPLAINED AS IN THE ORDER OF NATURE?

This is the place! Here the real life began! Christ indeed was born in Bethlehem, but Nazareth was the home of his mother, and hither, after the flight into Egypt, he was brought, still a child; here he grew, not only to boyhood but to manhood; and except his visits to Jerusalem at the annual feasts, it may almost be said that he knew no other world than that within the circuit of these hills.

That the greater part of the life of our Lord was passed at Nazareth (he was called a Nazarene), gives it an interest to the Christian traveller above all other places in Palestine, save perhaps Bethlehem where he was born, and Jerusalem where he was crucified. Of course, it is full of localities made sacred, in tradition if not in reality, by incidents of his life. Close to the spot where we camped is an old Greek church, called the Church of the Annunciation, on the site of which it is claimed that the angel appeared to Mary and announced to her that she should bear a son and call his name Jesus. The tradition is rejected by the Latins, who are not disposed to leave to the Greeks the honor, and the profit, of being the sole possessors of a site so sacred; and who have a church of their own, bearing the same name, and claiming to mark the same hallowed spot. /

Of course every traveller makes the round of these holy places—visiting the house of Mary and the carpenter's shop of Joseph, the site of the synagogue in which Jesus preached, and the brow of the hill from which they would cast him down. One who inquires into the genuineness of these sites, finds that there is little to support them. Thus this scene is transferred from its natural site, a cliff within the town, "whereon the city was built," to a lofty peak two miles away, which is called the Mount of Precipitation. But it is best not to inquire into these things too narrowly, or to waste time in sifting out a few grains of wheat from the chaff of tradition. Better to rest content with things about which there can be no dispute. At least the natural features of Nazareth remain unchanged. The hills which surround it are the same to which our Lord looked up from his mother's door. The centre of the ancient town was probably the Fountain which bears the Virgin's name, for in these Eastern villages the place to which all repair to draw water, is what the market place is in the little towns of Italy or of Germany. To this fountain still come the daughters of Nazareth, filling their large pitchers, or urns, from the full-flowing stream, and balancing them gracefully on their shoulders. No one can doubt that it is the same which flowed here two thousand years ago, and to which she whose name it now bears came a thousand times, often leading by the hand the wonderful child. /

With such associations and traditions, Nazareth has naturally attracted pilgrims, till it has become, like Bethlehem, a Christian town. There is not a Jew in Nazareth; there are Moslems, but the Christians are in large majority, and the superior character of the population is seen in the

better houses, which instead of being of mud, as in most
of the villages of Palestine, are of stone, and have at least
an appearance of solidity. The Christian community, as
usual in the East, is divided between the Greeks and the
Latins, though not in equal proportions, the Greeks being
much the more numerous, although the Latins to keep up
their rivalship, outdo the Greeks in architecture, their great
Franciscan Convent quite overshadowing the little town.

Apart from its sacred memories, Nazareth has nothing
to attract the eye of the traveller. The hills of Galilee are
indeed less barren than those of Judea. But the town
itself, or rather the village, has no beauty. Indeed, no
Eastern village has any beauty as compared with a village
of Old England, or of New England. How can a village
be pretty in which all the houses are of one uniform shape
and color? In an English village there is a variety of
construction, which saves it from the appearance of monotony. The country house stands on a green lawn, with
its central mass relieved from heaviness by its projecting
porch and shaded veranda and sloping roof, with here
and there angles and projections, casting shadows on its
sides. Here the houses have as much variety as so many
blocks of stone hewn out of a quarry. Each is a perfect
cube, " the length and the breadth and the height of it are
equal." The top of the house is square, like the foundation ; the roof is as flat as the floor. True, these flat roofs
serve a purpose in the East, where the oppressive heat
restrains the outdoor life of the people, who keep indoors
as much as they can in the heat of the day, but at night
go up on the housetops to enjoy the cooler air, and look
up into the unclouded heaven. Often they sleep on the
roofs, which are thus useful if not picturesque. /

The color, too, is not at all grateful to the eye. Built
of the limestone of the country, the houses are of such a

glaring white that it is painful to look upon them in the full blaze of the midday sun. This bareness is relieved only at one season of the year, in the Springtime, when the houses are partly hidden by the abundant vegetation ; by the gardens of olive and fig trees, and the vines that creep over the walls.

But the interest of Nazareth is not in its scenery so much as in its history : not its houses or its hills, but the fact that it was the cradle of our Religion, as it was the home of its Founder. As a town, it was in Galilee what Bethlehem was in Judah, "the least of its thousands." But it witnessed the beginning of a great history. In the Himalayas there is a stream which flows forth from under a glacier. It may be no more than others which issue from that region of eternal snow : but it is the source of the Ganges, a river which to hundreds of millions is like the River flowing out of the throne of God. So from this little mountain town of Galilee has gone forth a stream which has flowed into all the world, and had the greatest influence on the destinies of mankind.

Here our Saviour passed his childhood. And what was it? Was he like other children, fond of sports? This is quite possible. Perhaps he was not an only child ; although many Biblical scholars are of opinion that those who are spoken of as his brothers and sisters were his cousins, but even in that case there is no reason to doubt that he lived with them in the free and unrestrained intercourse of childhood. There is something very sweet in the thought that his early days were happy ; that he who was to suffer so much in life and in death, had at least a few years of brightness ; that this quiet valley was the place

> " Where once his careless childhood strayed,
>     A stranger yet to pain."

But it is difficult to think of his childhood as "careless," not only in the sense of thoughtless, but even in the lighter sense of being free from care. His question in the temple, "Wist ye not that I must be about my Father's business?" indicated that he was already beginning to feel the burden of responsibility. He was now twelve years of age. With such thoughts in his young heart, he was yet to wait eighteen years before the time of activity should come. In regard to this long period—more than half of his whole life — the Gospels are silent. He "increased in wisdom." But in what way?—by what influences?—under what teachers? Of all this the Scriptures say nothing. For him no doubt it was a period of preparation. But what a proportion between the period of preparation and that of action! The former was six times the latter. There is a lesson in this long seclusion, this apparent inactivity, which is a rebuke to our impatience to appear too early on the scene. We may well restrain our eagerness when we remember the patient waiting of our Master :

> God doth not need
> Either man's work, or his own gifts ;
> .   .   .   .   .   .   .   .   .
> They also serve who only stand and wait.

In the early centuries, and during the Middle Ages, the monks, who were never wanting in devices to feed popular superstition, filled up this large gap in the history of our Lord with childish legends. But so far as any authentic history goes, this portion of the life of Christ is veiled in absolute obscurity. /

But some modern writers who despise legends and traditions, take equal liberties in another way. Since they know nothing of the early life of our Lord, they gather from the histories of the time such general knowledge as

they can of the state of Galilee, from which they form an
opinion of the influences around him, and so construct a
theory of his "education," of the way in which he spent
the thirty years before he entered on his ministry.  The
sacred narrative tells us only that "he grew in stature"—
to physical manhood ; "and in wisdom," which may mean
in learning, in knowledge, or in moral elevation ; "and in
favor with God and man."  But they talk learnedly about
his studies and his masters and teachers.

Renan, the celebrated French author, has written a Life
of Jesus, which in some respects is a fascinating piece of
biography.  It is full of poetry and eloquence, and is written in a reverent spirit, although it rejects entirely what is
supernatural in the birth and in the life of our Lord.  He
believes him to have been born, not in Bethlehem, but in
Nazareth, and to have been the son of Joseph as well as of
Mary.  He does not admit that he was of the house of
David, and even questions his Hebrew descent, since at the
time that he was born, Galilee "had a very mixed population—not only Jews, but Phœnicians, Syrians, Arabs, and
even Greeks."  "It is impossible," says Renan, as if this
were to the honor of Jesus, "to raise any question of race,
and to search what blood flowed in the veins of him who
was to efface all distinctions of blood in a common human-
ity."  And yet this Being, sprung from he knows not what
race, he concedes to have been the greatest Personage of
whom history makes mention, and the establishment of
his religion the grandest event in the history of the world.

On this basis of pure naturalism he attempts to construct a Life of Jesus, but the attempt tries all his resources
of historical knowledge and subtle ingenuity.  How came
this wonderful character to appear in such a corner of the
world?  The ancient astrologers had a theory that great
human intellects were the product of celestial influences ;

that there was some conjunction of the stars that shone on their birth. But what was the conjunction of stars that wrought in producing this "grand soul"? Astronomers could easily tell us, reckoning backward to the year of our Saviour's birth. Was it "the sweet influences of Pleiades" that fell on the Galilean Hills? Was there one hour—one moment—in all the tide of time when the celestial influences combined to produce an intellect and a character of which there had been no example in history before? /

In place of the old astrologers has come in these days a generation of wise men, who account for everything by "nature." The heavens do not interfere with the course of human affairs; the earth alone is sufficient for her children. Everything extraordinary in the realm of intelligence is explained by "genius," a word which appears constantly in the pages of Renan, and which, if vague, is convenient, as it may be used to account for whatever one cannot understand. Such writers make light of "inspiration," but talk of "genius" as if it were something superhuman, if not divine—an effluence of intellectual force from the heart of nature, which, by influences celestial or terrestrial, is nourished to the height of intellectual greatness. The genius of Shakespeare was an extraordinary gift of nature, if not a direct inspiration of the Almighty. Those who trace its beginning and its growth, recognize the subtle, the invisible influences of nature, as in the well known sonnet to the Avon :

"In thy green lap was Nature's darling laid."

But in what "green lap" of nature was cradled the spirit of the young Hebrew? He was not the darling of nature or of fortune. He was not born on the banks of the Avon, but among the rugged Galilean hills.

No doubt, there is a wide difference in the constitutions

of men.  There are natures so delicately sensitive to spiritual influences, that they catch inspiration from the common
air which others breathe, but which in them works to no
such fine issues.  "What time the South wind blows, the
violets open their petals to the sun," and so there are certain influences which come from the very elements, which
touch the human soul and quicken it to life.  Such influences, the modern school of naturalists will have it, touched
and kindled the imagination of the child Jesus, dimly con-
scious of his transcendent powers, yet having nothing to
converse with but nature.  ("He always kept close to
nature," says Renan.)  It is easy to picture the "mar-
vellous boy" climbing the heights around Nazareth, and
looking with his great eyes upon what seemed to him the
boundless plain below, beyond which lay Jerusalem, the
capital of his country and his faith ; and off to the Sea
which rolled upon the horizon, the emblem of immensity,
. of infinity, and eternity.  And so in silence and communion with nature, his soul grew to its immeasurable greatness.

These are pleasing fancies with which historians and
philosophers entertain themselves.  What a pity that they
are mere creations of the brain, without a particle of
evidence to serve as a foundation for the airy superstructure.

But had not Christ masters and teachers?  Renan
devotes a whole chapter to the "education of Jesus," in
which out of the slenderest materials he weaves a theory
of the influences that may have reached him.  He makes
much of the intellectual activity of the time.  Jesus was
born in the Augustan age.  May not some influence from
Rome, or the philosophy of Greece, a country which was
much nearer, have reached the Eastern shore of the Mediterranean?  Possibly, but it would have affected only the

learned and the great. It is hardly possible that it could have reached a little mountain town of Galilee. In all the teachings of Christ there appears not once the slightest evidence that he had so much as heard of Rome, except as the seat of the Empire of Cæsar. And indeed if any influence could have come from the West, so full of skepticism and materialism was the philosophy of that age, that it would have been positively unfavorable to moral, if not to intellectual, growth. ✓

But what he did not learn from the wise men of Greece, may he not have learned from teachers of his own race, " devout men who were waiting for the consolation of Israel"? No doubt the child of Mary was taught in the faith of her fathers. In that humble home there was a strong Hebrew spirit, which was nourished by the words of seers and prophets. May he not have sat at the feet of learned rabbis, as Paul sat at the feet of Gamaliel? We are told of certain Jewish sects which existed in the time of Christ, particularly the Essenes, who taught many things which are in striking accordance with the precepts of our Lord. "It may be supposed," says Renan, "that the principles of Hillel were not unknown to him. Hillel, fifty years before, had pronounced aphorisms which had much analogy with his. By his poverty meekly borne, by the mildness of his character, by the opposition he made to the hypocrites and the priests, Hillel was the true master of Christ, if it be permitted to speak of a master of one who had so high an originality." By this kind of loose reasoning, "supposing" that of which he has no evidence, Renan arrives virtually at the conclusion that there was a Christianity before Christ ; that he merely put it into a more complete form, crystallizing elements which had long been in solution in the Hebrew mind.

This is a very ingenious theory ; nothing is wanting

but that it should be true.  But unfortunately there is not
the slightest evidence that Christ belonged to the sect of
the Essenes, or was taught in the school of Hillel.  Had it
been so, would not a nature so simple, so transparent and
sincere, as Christ's is confessed to have been, have made
some acknowledgment to his masters and teachers? instead
of which he always spoke in his own name, even setting
aside the authority of Moses and the prophets.  The
theory of " education " fails as utterly as that of " genius."
The greatest teachers could not give what they did not
possess.  The distance is so immense between anything
discovered in the teachings of ancient rabbis and the
teaching of Christ, that it is impossible to suppose one
derived from the other.  And so the elaborate theory of
Renan, on which he has constructed the life of Christ,
breaks down at every point.  Indeed if the appeal be to
history, it may be shown that the age of Christ was
unfriendly to the new faith.  The Jews looked for a temporal deliverer, but a spiritual teacher they were never
less fitted to receive.  As a people, they were narrow and
bigoted to an extreme—counting that they only were the
people of God, and that all others were accursed.  Those
who claimed to be the most righteous, were the most
oppressive and cruel, putting heavy burdens on others'
shoulders, but not touching them with one of their fingers.
From such a soil sprang the consummate flower of virtue.
Out of ignorance came forth wisdom ; out of pride came
forth meekness ; out of selfishness and cruelty came forth
a love which embraced all mankind.  Was this a " natural "
result of a "natural" cause ?  Believe it who will.  All the
subtle explanations in the world cannot account for the
Christ on the principles of naturalism.  The appearance of
such a Being was *not* in the course of nature ; it was supernatural.  The more I travel in these Eastern countries—

the more I see of the Jews—the more do I feel that to suppose Jesus Christ to be a natural product of such a race and such an age, is to suppose a greater miracle than to accept his divinity.

Such doubts do not trouble me here. In the region where our Lord passed the greater part of his life, the whole story of the Gospels is so real, it fits so into the very landscape, it has so perfectly the *couleur locale* of the hills and valleys, that one passing through them cannot but recognize the literal truth of all in the New Testament which pertains to things external. Accepting this, one soon accepts the supernatural also ; and instead of puzzling his brain with explanations which do not explain, and theories which are mere guesses at truth, he accepts the simple affirmation of the Apostles' Creed, that Jesus Christ "was conceived by the Holy Ghost and born of the Virgin Mary."

Such reflections occur naturally to one spending a Sabbath in Nazareth. But the day is passing, and before it closes let us go out to take one more view of a region so familiar to the eye and the footsteps of our Lord. In the rear of our camp, forming a background for the little town, is a hill which rises five hundred feet above the valley below. Towards the close of the day we climbed to the top, as on a memorable Sabbath in the desert, in the Oasis of Feiran, we had climbed the hill where Moses knelt while Hur and Aaron held up his hands till the going down of the sun. On the highest point is an ancient Wely or Moslem tomb, and clambering over the stones, we perched ourselves on its arched roof, where we sat down to take a survey of the country. There are few points in Palestine which command a more extensive view. Below us lay the village of Nazareth, shut in by its guardian hills. Beyond and around it stretched the great plain of Esdraëlon. On the West the sun was sinking behind the ridge of Carmel into the Western Sea, while northward Hermon reared his lofty head against the sky, his crown of snow flushed with warmer tints as it caught the rays of the setting sun. It was a scene of enchantment. Could we doubt that the Master had a thousand times climbed to this very spot, to look round the same horizon?

On the side of this hill, half way down the descent, stands one of the noblest institutions in Palestine, for the instruction of orphan girls. Established by the English Female Education Society, it is one of those monuments which one finds everywhere in the East, and for that matter everywhere in the world, of the Christian liberality of England. It is under the charge of an English lady, Miss Dickson, who received us kindly, and took us through the large building, in which we could not but admire the completeness of the recitation rooms and dormitories, and all the appointments, which were such as might be looked for in a Model School of England or America. At last she led us to an upper hall, where, seated on benches rising one behind the other, were perhaps a hundred children, whom she asked to sing us a hymn. They had learned a little English, and at once began the familiar lines :

> " What means this eager, anxious throng,
> Which moves with busy haste along—
> These wondrous gatherings day by day ?
> What means this strange commotion, pray ?
> In accents hushed the throng reply,
> *Jesus of Nazareth passeth by.*"

These words would have been pleasant to hear anywhere ; but they were peculiarly touching in Nazareth, and from the lips of children. The soft melody seemed to be still in the air as we descended the long flight of steps, and made our way down the hillside to our camp. It was in sweet and tender harmony with the place and the hour. Though the day was nearly gone, the golden light still lingered on the heights above us, where in the last glow of sunset seemed to float the form of Him who once walked among these hills. Was not the Master "passing by"? Does he not love to revisit the scenes dear to him on earth? May he not often return to the spot where he spent the greater part of his mortal life? Perhaps he still loves these hours when the last light of day is fading round his early home. So at least it seemed to us, whether it was faith or imagination : to the quickened sense he was very near ; it was as if we could see him dimly in the twilight, nay, as if he who came to his disciples when the door was shut, and said "Peace be unto you," stood within the door of our tent, and gave his peace to those who, though strangers and pilgrims, were yet his disciples. Jesus of Nazareth *was* passing by.

# CHAPTER XII.

/ In the preface to Kenilworth, Walter Scott tells how he came to write it. The idea was suggested by an old English ballad, which he heard when a young man. "The first stanza especially," he says, "had a peculiar species of enchantment for the youthful ear of the author, the force of which is not even now entirely spent." This we can well believe as we read these musical lines :

> " The dews of Summer night did fall;
> The moon, sweet regent of the sky,
> Silvered the walls of Cumnor Hall,
> And many an oak that grew thereby."

Repeating these lines a thousand times, he finally wrote this romance of the time of Elizabeth, as if to reproduce the effect of the moonlight falling on castle walls, and silvering the ancient oaks. If a few lines may thus set in motion the pen of a great writer, much more are travellers, who are like ships in that they are always afloat, turned about with " the very small helm " of a slight association. A bit of eloquent description, whether in poetry or prose, haunts the mind and makes one travel far to place himself in the situation, and realize the effect, so powerfully described. It was something like this which made at least one member of our party wish to turn aside from the direct journey through Palestine, to visit Mount Carmel. When Dean Stanley was in America, he preached a sermon in Stockbridge, Mass., on a text which certainly promised little. It was "There is nothing!"—the exclamation of the servant whom Elijah sent up to the top of Mount Carmel to look towards the Mediterranean, to see if there were any sign of rain, and who returned again and again with the same answer : "There is nothing!" At first one would think there could be nothing to a sermon from such a text. But it soon appeared that out of "nothing" the genius of such a preacher could draw most important lessons. I can see now the slight figure, with that intellectual countenance, and hear his voice as he began : /

In the story of Elijah on Mount Carmel, there is a striking passage—made to some of us yet more striking by the music of Mendelssohn, in which it has been enshrined—where the young lad attendant on the Prophet ascends the highest point of the long ridge of the mountain, and whilst his master remains on the lower level, looks out over the wide expanse of the Mediterranean Sea. It is a scene of which every step can still be identified. The boy gazes in the hope that the Prophet's earnest prayer may bring down the long-desired rain. The sun had sunk into the western sea. But after the sunset there followed the long white glow so common in the evenings of Eastern countries. Seven times the youthful watcher went up and looked, and seven times he reported "There is nothing." The sky was still clear; the sea was still calm. At last out of the far horizon there arose a little cloud, the first that for days and months had passed across the heavens. It was no larger than an outstretched hand, but it grew in the deepening shades of evening, and quickly the whole sky was overcast, and the forests of Carmel shook in the welcome sound of those mighty winds which in Eastern regions precede a coming tempest. The cry of the boy from his mountain watch had hardly been uttered when the storm broke upon the plain, the rain descended, the Kishon swelled and burst over its banks, and the nation was delivered from its sufferings.

This eloquent passage remained in my memory till I found myself in Palestine, and raised a strong desire, as we approached Carmel, to visit the mountain and recall "the scene of which every step can still be identified," and look out, like the servant of Elijah, " over the wide expanse of the Mediterranean Sea."/

The day smiled on our purpose, for we had not had in all our journeys a more exquisite morning. With a long ride before us, we were in the saddle at six o'clock. To climb up out of the basin of Nazareth, we wound round the steep hill in the rear of our camp which we had ascended the evening before. The sun had just risen over the mountains of Gilead, on the other side of the Jordan, and touched the forehead of Tabor, and as we rose higher, it shone down into the valley below. Descending the other slope of the hill to the plain of Esdraelon, we soon had a view of Haifa and Acre in the distance, on the shore of the Mediterranean. It is perhaps not more than a dozen miles directly across to the foot of Carmel, though by the circuitous route we had to take, it must have been much farther. The road was wet with the recent rains, but the horses, fresh from a day of rest, pricked up their steps, and we measured off the distance rapidly. The plain is not altogether level, but rising and falling, with here and there a larger swell of ground, on which is the usual Eastern village—a cluster of mud-huts, no better than Indian wigwams, with the smoke pouring out of the door ; yet through the smoke, as if they were imps of darkness, peer innumerable heads : for these miserable cabins swarm with men and women, children and dogs. Once only in the whole distance did we see a building of any size, and that was erected as a khan for the Circassians, who made it little better than a robbers' castle. Just now it is empty, and looks like an old barrack which has been deserted and \

gone to ruin. The traveller is surprised at the desolate appearance of the country, so far as regards human habitation. The soil is rich, and if the plain were thoroughly cultivated, as it would be in England, or as are the Lowlands of Scotland, or the reclaimed marshes of Holland, it would support the whole population of Palestine. But it sadly lacks the presence of man and the benefit of human industry. The villages are the poorest and the people the most wretched in the country. The reason is not far to seek : it is the insecurity of life and property. If one looks on the map, he will see that the Plain of Esdraelon does not lie four-square in the heart of the country, but runs across it from northwest to southeast, touching the Mediterranean on one side and the valley of the Jordan on the other. The smooth descent to the latter opens a wide gate for the entrance of the Bedaween, who in former years came in by thousands with their flocks and herds. They considered the plain of Esdraelon as their pasture ground, and that no others had any rights which they were bound to respect. Where they came, it was hardly possible for others to live. They turned the cultivated field into a desert, since their hand was against every man, and every man's hand was against them. Until within a few years it was said that only a sixth part of the soil was cultivated at all. Since 1870 it is claimed that the protection has been somewhat better. Yet I do not see the signs of improvement. The plain indeed overflows with rank vegetation, but there is little culture. If the inrush of Bedaween has been less than in former years, at least the apprehension remains, and the terror has the effect to keep the land desolate. Out of the villages the plain is uninhabited. Here and there men or boys may be seen watching a few sheep or cattle, but otherwise it is as silent and solitary as the desert. It is not safe for any one to travel alone, even

armed : indeed arms sometimes but increase the danger.
As we came near a village, Floyd pointed out a spot where
only four years since a young Englishman, the son of a
nobleman, who had lived in the country long enough to
feel a certain degree of security, was attacked, and endeavoring to defend himself with his revolver, was overpowered
and killed, and his body cut into three pieces! Of course
the heart of England was stirred at such a crime, and a
man-of-war, with the English Consul from Jerusalem on
board, was ordered to Acre to demand satisfaction. Sixty
men of the village were arrested, and an inquest begun
which lasted twenty-six days, as the result of which three
who were found to have been leaders in the crime, were
sentenced to be hanged. Sentenced, but not executed!
They were confined in the fortress of Acre, where they still
are, unless they have been allowed to escape! So much
for Turkish justice. /

Three hours of riding brought us to the Kishon, which,
like many things in the East, is an uncertain quantity,
being now a brook and now a river. Sometimes it is
almost dry ; but fearing lest it might be swollen by the
recent rains, Floyd made anxious inquiry, as we approached it, if it was fordable. On the banks we found
boys watching cattle, which were wading and wallowing
under the willows ; and a man was sent in to see if the
water was too deep. Following him, we rode in and
waded across. It is a narrow stream, and we can hardly
understand how it could have swept away the host of
Sisera. But in these Eastern countries the elements, like
the people, are treacherous ; and when the rains descend,
the brook becomes a flood, rushing through the plain like
a mountain torrent, and might easily sweep away an army./

And now we begin to ascend, and from gentle slopes
soon come to the wooded sides of Carmel, which is cele-

brated for its flora.* The springs which run among the hills keep it always fresh and green. The contrast with the barren hills over which we had passed in other parts of Palestine and on the desert, gave it a peculiar beauty. After being so long among the bald peaks of the Peninsula of Sinai, it was a relief to the eye to come into something like an American forest. The sides of the mountain are covered with trees. Isaiah, who was prophet and poet in one, couples "the excellency of Carmel and Sharon" with "the glory of Lebanon." Its forest growths attracted the priests of Baal, who celebrated their idolatrous worship in its sacred groves. An hour's ride up the ascent brought us to a place where is a fountain welling up among the rocks, at the foot of a ledge perhaps twenty feet high. Mounting this ledge, we come upon a broad natural terrace, which is supposed to be the scene of the memorable contest of Elijah with the prophets of Baal, as the space is ample for thousands to gather round the altars, while the water to pour into the trenches could be brought from the fountain below. With these accessories before the eye, it is easy to picture the scene. The Scriptures hardly contain anything more dramatic than the description of a contest which ended in a fearful tragedy. The people were probably gathered by tens of thousands, for Elijah had bidden Ahab "send and gather all Israel unto Mount Carmel." The multitude may have covered the whole

* My friend and companion in travel, Dr. Adams, who is always observant of trees and flowers, notes in his journal a few of those which here caught his eye: "Going up Carmel saw wild hollyhocks large and fine; three varieties of clover (large red, large white, small red blossoms); white and red rock-roses; oaks and hawthorns; and mock-orange trees (or syringas) from ten to twenty feet high, in full blossom perfuming the air." On the very top of the mountain I observed the same profusion of wild flowers and blossoming trees, whose fragrance was like a breath of home./

mountain side, and stretched far out into the plain below. But the scene of the conflict was near the crest of the mountain, on the terrace, where were assembled the leaders of the people, while in the foreground appeared hundreds of the priests of Baal. Their altars are built and their prayers begin, but as no effect is produced, they soon work themselves into a state of excitement—an excitement which passes into fury and frenzy. They shout like howling dervishes, making the forest echo with their cries, "O Baal, hear us!" This they repeat from morning to noon, and after noon, growing more wild and frantic, leaping upon the altar and cutting themselves with knives till the blood gushes out upon them, but at last sink down from utter exhaustion, obliged to confess their failure, and only hoping that the prophet of the Lord may fail also.

Then Elijah stood forth, one man, alone, against the hundreds of the prophets of Baal, and said unto all the people, Come near unto me! With a solemn deliberation he repairs the altar of the Lord that was broken down, and digs a trench and bids them pour barrels of water on the sacrifice, and again bids them do it the second time, and do it the third time.

"Then at the time of the evening sacrifice Elijah came near and said, Lord God of Abraham, of Isaac, and of Israel, Let it be known this day that thou art God in Israel, and that I am thy servant, and that I have done all these things according to thy word." "Then the fire of the Lord fell and consumed the burnt sacrifice and the wood and the stones and the dust, and licked up the water that was in the trench."/

The victory was complete, and the retribution came. In one of those revulsions of feeling that follow a discovered deception, the people responded quickly to the command to "seize the prophets of Baal, not to let one of them escape," and they were taken down the mountain, and slain on the banks of the Kishon, which rolled red with their blood to the sea.

But we are not yet quite at the summit of Carmel; there is still a cliff some three hundred feet higher. As we climb to the top there bursts upon us a view of mountain and sea close to each other, not unlike that from the Corniche road in the South of France, or from Amalfi in Italy. The ridge of Carmel is about eighteen miles long, on either side of which the deep green of the forest slopes down to the plain—on one side to the Plain of Esdraelon, and on the other to the Plain of Sharon, which coming up from the South along the coast, here grows narrower and narrower till it is lost between the mountain and the sea. Carmel ends abruptly with a sharp descent. This headland jutting out into the deep is the most striking object seen by the voyager along the Syrian coast. On the extreme point, nearly five hundred feet above the sea, stands the famous monastery which has given name to the order of Barefooted Carmelites so well known throughout Europe—an order to which Father Hyacinthe once belonged. From this commanding elevation one may look North, South, and West, and see in each direction the illimitable sea. Lying almost at our feet, like the Bay of Salerno as seen from the heights of the Appenines, is the Bay of Acre, over which still keeps guard that ancient fortress, before which Napoleon met with a defeat which stopped his conquest of Syria and his march upon Constantinople.*/

* While I was looking seaward, Dr. Adams had been looking back over the plain, and thus pictures the wonderful scene in that direction: "We go to the edge of a forty-foot cliff of pumice rock. Dr. Field reads the Scripture [1 Kings xviii.]. Looking off over the plain, we see all the sites of the story,

As the point we had now reached is the highest of the mountain, tradition has naturally fixed upon it as the scene of Elijah's victory, and there is a small low building of stone covering a bare rock, which is claimed to have been the very rock of sacrifice. But a careful comparison of sites inclines to the broader space below. It is, however, not improbable that this higher peak was the watch-tower from which Elijah's servant looked for the cloud from the sea. After the prophets of Baal had been slain at the brook Kishon, it is said that "Elijah went up to the top of Carmel"; but it may be only in a general sense, for he sent his servant up to a point still higher, so that it seems probable that he renewed his prayer on the very spot where he had already been answered by fire from heaven. His prayer was perhaps a silent one, for we are told only that "he cast himself upon the earth and put his face between his knees." But voiceless though it was, he did not doubt that the answer would come, for he bade his servant look for its coming : "Go up now, look toward the sea!" Nor did his faith fail, though again and again the servant reported "There is nothing," for at the seventh time, he answered "Behold, there ariseth a little cloud out of the sea, like a man's hand." And soon "the heaven was black with clouds and wind, and there was a great rain."/

Such is the story of the prophet that hangs about the ridge of Carmel, and gives it an interest after the lapse of nearly thirty centuries. What strange and terrible power had these men, who dwelt in mountains and caves, and came out of their solitude to stand before kings and send

with Jezreel in the distance; grass greens in various shades, earth browns and blacks, the winding thread of the Kishon; on the Galilean hills tree greens and limestone grays; far away purples and blues, and the snows of Hermon."/

terror into palaces! The prophets are dead, but their memory lingers in the haunted air ; something of their fierce spirit seems to have entered into the very eagles that still soar and scream above the heights of Carmel, sending out their wild message to mountain and sea. /

As we rode down Mount Carmel, the afternoon sun behind us shone across Esdraelon, bringing out every mound and knoll of that most beautiful plain. Some of the broader elevations are studded with noble trees, making a landscape not unlike the parks of England ; and one looks to see castle walls behind the ancient oaks, or something having the charm of an English village under their shade. Such there might be, if there were only the order and security of England. The plain itself is nature's paradise. It is a sea of verdure ; for, cultivated or not, whether in gardens or overgrown with weeds, still the rank luxuriant growth gives it the appearance of one of our Western prairies, and suggests what it might become with proper cultivation. But there cannot be good cultivation without good government. Just now I was riding by the side of Floyd, when we met a couple of " gentlemen," splendidly mounted and armed. We gave them our salaam, which they returned. But Floyd smiled as he said "If you were alone, instead of being with a party, these knights of the road would pay you closer attention. They would give you the honor of a personal interview." This is the curse of the country ; no man is safe either on the road or in his dwelling : his home is not his castle. The poor peasant has no motive to cultivate a garden or plant a tree, for the moment that he makes his little place attractive, it is sure to become the prey of the spoiler. /

As if it were not enough that this beautiful Plain should be overrun by hordes of Bedaween, the Sultan has emptied upon it a body of Circassians. At the close of the late war there were hordes of irregular troops—Koords, Bashi-bazouks and Circassians—a horrible set of cut-throats, useless in war, as they were subject to no discipline, and only intent on pillage—whom it was necessary to get rid of, and whom the government wished to send as far away as possible. Some of them were transported into the interior of Asia Minor. Wherever they came they were a pest to every village, as they were a set of thieves and robbers. A large detachment of these precious scoundrels were landed on the Coast of Syria and encamped on the Plain of Esdraelon, to be the terror of their neighbors.

Thus the land is doomed to desolation, for nothing can stand against such a state of insecurity. How long would the farmers of Illinois plant their magnificent prairies if there were roving bands of Indians, or of "bushwhackers," too powerful to be resisted, that would come in as soon as the harvest was ripe to take whatever was best—to turn their herds of horses and cattle into the rich pastures, staying for weeks or months and leaving only when the land was swept as a prairie is swept by fire?

Whenever we meet, as we often do, these roving Bedaween, it renews our conversation in regard to the state of a country which is thus given over to brigandage.

Floyd has lived many years in Palestine, and travelling in every part of it, he has become well acquainted with the different tribes that inhabit the country across the Jordan, and with their sheikhs, who converse with him with the greatest freedom. Sitting before their camp-fires, they are in a confidential mood, and as they like to unbosom themselves to an admiring listener, they do not hesitate to boast of their exploits. It is a feather in the cap of a sheikh to be a bold marauder. He who can plan a raid upon his neighbors, and carry it out with secrecy and despatch, is a great man in his tribe. And if in executing some feat of strategy, he and his "merry men" come to battle and to blood, this gives increased zest to their wild and lawless life. The sheikh of a powerful tribe beyond the Jordan has a daughter who is famed for her beauty ; but the sheikh gives it to be understood that no young Arabian "blood" must look for her hand who has not killed a hundred men! What a noble object to fire a young Arab's ambition! This, of course, must be in pitched battle : for the Arabs do not like assassination. Killing, to be a matter of pride, must be done on a large scale.

In pursuing their knightly calling, they are sometimes *obliged* to kill those whom they rob. They would rather not do this : for they do not like to shed blood, having a wholesome fear of the blood feud. But they have no moral scruple about it. Sometimes when stern necessity compels a murder, one may feel a slight twinge of remorse. "One day," said a sheikh to Floyd, "as I was riding across a plain, I saw coming towards me a man mounted on the most beautiful mare I had ever seen [the Arabian mares are especially prized] ; her form was perfect ; there was such grace and spirit in every step, that I turned to look at her with admiration, when an impulse seized me which I could not resist. It was the work of an instant. I dashed at the rider, and ran him through with my spear. He rolled off, but gave me one look that I could never forget. I should have thought nothing of the act but for that last look : but that has haunted me ever since. It follows me to my tent, and when I awake in the night, I see those eyes staring at me with a look of reproach. But," he always adds, "*who could help it for such a mare !*"

This wild element is the most difficult one to manage in the whole Empire. Some indeed think it impossible to control it. The Bedaween have roamed the desert for thousands of years unsubdued, and may still roam for thousands of years to come. They snap their fingers at a power as far off as Constantinople, and speak with the utmost contempt of the Turks. Floyd told me how a sheikh shook his fist and fairly gnashed his teeth at the mention of the Sultan. "He wished he had the Sultan *here*," intimating by gesture as well as by words that he would run his spear through the sacred body of the Padisha. Such refractory sheikhs are not easily made into faithful and obedient subjects ; and it can hardly be wondered at if the Grand Vizier, sitting on his legs, and smoking his chibouque, and not wishing to be disturbed, gives it up as a bad job.

But because the Turks cannot subdue these wild tribes of the desert, it does not follow that they cannot be subdued by any power. The best proof that they can be, is that *they have been*. It is not so long ago that the present generation should forget that there was a time when Ibrahim Pasha invaded Palestine and Syria. For ten years he was master of the country, and he *governed* it. The Arabs soon found that they had a master. A few prompt executions, a few sheikhs swung in air, and a few villages destroyed, and the idea was fairly driven into their rebellious heads, that they were dealing with a ruler who could not be trifled with. "In those days," said Dr. Van Dyck of Beirut, "you did not need a guard if you stepped out of doors, or passed from village to village ; you could travel in safety from one end of the land to the other."

This was the first time in centuries that Syria had been governed. But such a state of things was too blissful to last. England and France, true to their policy of upholding Turkey, and fearful lest the Egyptian army should march on Constantinople, must interfere, and in another siege of Acre stopped Ibrahim Pasha as Sir Sidney Smith had stopped Napoleon. Ibrahim was compelled to give up

his hold on Syria and retreat to Egypt, and at once the
old anarchy came back again, and still continues, with no
hope of being destroyed till some other power than Turkey
shall become master of the country, whether it obtain it by
war or peace, by conquest or by civilization.

"Civilization?" What civilization can there be amid
so much barbarism? At present the only sign of civilization is the little wire which runs along the line of telegraph
poles. But that slender wire is the nerve that links three
continents together. Starting from Cairo, and crossing the
desert to Jaffa and Jerusalem, it unites Asia to Africa ; and
then circling round the head of the Mediterranean, reaches
Constantinople, and there touches the great system of
communication which spreads over Europe. This wire
therefore is not so slight a thing as it seems : it is the fore-
runner of civilization—a sign of greater things which are
to follow. /

Of one of these there is a suggestion already in the proposed construction of "the first railway in Palestine"!
For a year past there have been rumors of a negotiation
on the part of bankers in Beirut, probably with the aid of
bankers in Constantinople, as the result of which it is
finally announced that the Sultan—in consideration of a
handsome royalty, equivalent to a large land tax—has
leased to them the Plain of Esdraelon, with the condition
that he shall protect it from the incursions of the Bedaween ; and that, as a part of the agreement, they receive a
concession for a railway. Accordingly they propose to
turn their large acquisition to account by the construction
of a railway from Acre to Damascus, which would strike
directly across the Plain of Esdraelon. It is suggested
that there might be a station for Nazareth (!), though it
would pass twelve miles south of the town, which might be
approached still nearer by a branch road to the foot of the

Galilean Hills ; while the main line, descending the valley of Jezreel, would "pass over Jordan," near an old Roman bridge, part of which is still standing and in use. Mr. Laurence Oliphant, an authority in all matters relating to the East, writing from Haifa, says : "Near this ancient Roman bridge of three arches, which is used to this day by the caravans of camels which bring the produce of the Hauran to the coast, the new railway bridge will cross the Jordan, probably the only one in the world which will have for its neighbor an actual bridge in use which was built by the Romans—thus, in this new, semi-barbarous country, bringing into close contact an ancient and a modern civilization." From the point of crossing the Jordan, the railway would keep along its bank till it diverged farther to the East to skirt the hills that rise on the shore of the Sea of Galilee. In its route to Damascus, it would traverse the Hauran, one of the richest agricultural regions in the East, the produce of which, no longer borne on the backs of camels, could now be carried, not only more swiftly, but in immensely greater bulk [one freight train would transport more than a dozen caravans] to the Mediterranean./

This would be indeed a commercial revolution in the Holy Land. But that is not the end. Still grander projects have been suggested, such as that of a canal which should rival the Suez Canal, or of a longer railroad, which should furnish another route to India besides that through Egypt. The late war awakened England to the absolute necessity, in order to preserve her Indian Empire, of a means of communication with it which cannot be interrupted or destroyed. While it is proposed to construct a second Suez Canal, the question is asked if there may not be another water-way from the Mediterranean to the Red Sea ; and engineers searching along the coast of Syria have suggested that it would be possible to make another

Port Said at Haifa, just above the head of Mount Carmel, from which a canal might be carried across the Plain of Esdraelon to the Jordan, and down its valley to the Dead Sea, from which a canal could be cut across the desert to Akaba, where it would strike the other arm of the Red Sea from that reached by the Suez Canal./

Such a line it is easy to draw on the map, but to the execution of the project there is one great natural difficulty, in the depression of the Dead Sea, which is thirteen hundred feet below the level of the Mediterranean. The same difficulty would not be experienced in constructing a railroad, which, if not as effective for commerce, would answer equally well for subduing and civilizing the country. Before the Bedaween can be civilized they must be governed ; and to be governed they must be subdued ; and to be subdued they must be reached. The first thing is to get at them. An army cannot be transported across the desert on camels. The Arabs would fly faster than the army could follow, only to return as soon as it was gone. But with a railroad reaching to the Gulf of Akaba, troops could easily be transported to within striking distance of the most powerful tribes. As the Pacific railroads are settling the Indian question, so railroads across the desert may yet settle the Arab question. /

But the project of a canal is the more captivating to the imagination, and it is hard to say to modern engineers that anything is impossible. This is an age of the world when the wildest anticipations of the past are exceeded by the realities of the present, and when it is but in the natural course of things, that young men should dream dreams and old men should see visions. It would seem indeed like a dream of prophecy fulfilled, if we could see the ships of modern commerce gathering on that coast from which the ancient Phenicians carried commerce and civilization to Greece and Italy and Spain ; and passing under the shadow of Carmel, enter the calm waters of an artificial river, and unfold their sails, the white wings of peace, over a plain which has been for ages the battle-field of nations ; then dropping slowly down into the Valley of the Jordan, and crossing the Plain of Jericho, (from which, but for the depression, the voyager might see the domes and towers of Jerusalem,) pass through the Dead Sea, under the shadow of the mountains of Moab, and over the buried cities of the Plain, without disturbing the dead of Sodom and Gomorrah ; and moving silently as "painted ships upon a painted ocean," across the solemn stillness of the desert, come at last to Akaba, and make a port of the ancient Ezion-geber, from which sailed the fleets of Solomon ! What a dream ! Yet this may be, for things more wonderful have been. By some such means perhaps the Eastern question is to be solved. May we not at least hope for it, and look for it ? Is it presumption to pray that this generation may not pass away until this dream shall be fulfilled ? /

# CHAPTER XIII.

TO TIBERIAS—THE SERMON ON THE MOUNT: IS IT
PHILOSOPHY, OR GENIUS, OR DIVINITY?

/ It was Tuesday morning when we struck our tents at
Nazareth, where we had been camped since Saturday. In
that time a place becomes familiar, and we have a home
feeling about it that makes us leave it with regret. It was
with a tender feeling that we turned to look for the last
time at the peaceful valley where our Lord was a child;
where he lived with his virgin mother. But the scene, like
childhood itself, must be left behind, that we may pass on
to other scenes connected not with the childhood, but with
the manhood, of him who is the Master of us all.

The hill up which we were now riding was the same
which we climbed yesterday; but as we passed over its
shoulder, instead of turning westward towards Mount Carmel, we kept northeast in the direction of the Lake of
Galilee, and soon came to places associated with the Old
Testament and the New. Here on our left, perched on a
high, steep hill, was the ancient Gath Hepher, the birth-
place of the prophet Jonah; and next we rode into a little
village, which Floyd announced with a loud voice to be
Cana of Galilee. As usual with these villages, it is clus-
tered about a fountain. "And this is the very fountain

from which the water was taken that was turned into wine!" This was so positive that it seemed as if it must be authentic, and I sprang from my horse, and stooping down, plunged my face into the brimming pool, and took a long draught. Some maidens, who had come to fill their pitchers with water, were "sitting on the well," and smiled, as I thought, at my enthusiasm ; but Floyd said they were laughing at the cut of my whiskers, for which I do not blame them : for there must be something very unimposing, not to say ridiculous, in our close-cropped hair to those accustomed to see the human countenance invested with dignity, and even made venerable, by the flowing Oriental beard. |

After the warmth with which I hailed this sacred spot, it was a little chilling to be told that it was not without a rival ; that there was another village of the same name not far away, which Robinson and other learned investigators believed to be the true Cana of Galilee. But I was not willing to give it up, for had I not been to the very house where the marriage feast was celebrated, and seen the very "water-pots" (huge earthen jars) in which the water stood which was converted into wine ? It is not to be supposed that this little village would willingly surrender its only title to fame. The tradition is its capital. Accordingly, there is a Greek priest on hand, gracious and smiling, (whether at the credulity of pilgrims or at the money he receives,) who unlocks the door, and shows the interior, with as little question of its genuineness as does the custodian of Independence Hall, who shows the original Declaration, with its immortal signatures. /

But whether the site of Cana can be identified or not, this at least is certain, that we are in Galilee, the scene of our Lord's ministry, at the beginning of which, "when John was cast into prison, he departed into Galilee, and leaving Nazareth came and dwelt in Capernaum, which is by the sea, in the borders of Zebulon and Naphtali." In going from Nazareth to Capernaum, he must have crossed these very hills and passed through these very valleys, all of which are hallowed by association with him. These associations gave a charm to that morning's ride, and when it came to the hour of noon, and we halted in the shade for our midday rest, I sat down at the foot of a tree and took out my Bible, and read chapter after chapter of the Gospel narrative. How real it all seems when one has the very landscape in his eye, as a background of the sacred story! /

But now we are coming to a spot which makes us pause and linger. It was the middle of the afternoon that we were riding across an upland at the slow and even pace into which travellers are apt to drop, when Floyd bounded ahead, and dashed up the side of a hill, which rises out of the plain. We followed, and when we had reined up beside him, he said "This is the Mount of the Beatitudes! Here Christ delivered the Sermon on the Mount!" Its identity rests upon tradition, but in this case tradition is so supported by natural probability, that cautious investigators accept it as genuine. I dismounted with the feeling that I ought to take my shoes off my feet: for this was holy ground. The mount itself is not indeed imposing. At first I was disappointed, as it seemed wanting in majesty. A few weeks before I had stood upon Mount Sinai, from which the Law was given amid thunderings and lightnings; but here the mount almost sinks down into the plain. Was this intended to symbolize the difference between the Law and the Gospel : that we were not come to the mount that burned with fire—to blackness and darkness and tempest—but to *a mount that might be touched*, with no barrier between us and our Master, to forbid our coming to his very feet? The formation of the ground is peculiar. It is not a rounded summit, but if we may use a familiar expression, "saddle-backed," with rising points at either end, which have given it the name of the Horns of Hattin. Between these "horns" is a small plateau, to which Christ is supposed to have descended when he "came down into the plain." This plateau is the bed of an old crater. To think that Christ should have preached the Sermon on the Mount on the crater of an extinct volcano! But the gulf through which once flamed the internal fires, is filled up now, and grass waves over the buried ashes.

Walking over the ground to this point and that, looking off in every direction, I perceived that, though as seen from the high plain to the west by which we approached, "the mount" is only a gentle elevation, yet that it has a commanding position relative to the surrounding country, as it stands alone, on an upland, from which it has an unbroken horizon, not being "dominated" by any higher eminence in its immediate vicinity. In full view, nearly two thousand feet below, lies the Sea of Galilee, with mountains all round it, far and near, whose sides are turned towards this central position. But in the foreground is nothing but this little plateau, which descends so gently that thousands might be stretched on the grassy slopes. Here then we may "rest awhile," as if taking a seat with the multitude that once spread over this very ground, to listen to words such as never fell from human lips before. /

The Sermon on the Mount is the most remarkable discourse of our Lord that has been preserved to us. As we are travelling, not merely for sight-seeing but for instruction, we cannot pass by this sacred spot, any more than by the Mount of Olives or the Garden of Gethsemane, without pausing to reflect on the lessons given to the world. Here, as at Nazareth, we have an opportunity to study Christianity on the spot where it began, and may be able to judge if it can be " explained," according to Renan, on natural principles, or on some theory of moral " evolution"; or we are compelled to admit that there is in it something which is supernatural and divine.

"And he went up into a mountain, and when he was set his disciples came unto him." So simply does the record begin. The sermon was addressed, first of all, to his disciples, but in another sense, to the whole world. The mount, though so modest in itself, was in the very focus of a wide region of country. Standing in the centre of a vast circumference, it seemed to be in the sight of all Galilee, and Galilee was then one of the most populous provinces of the Roman Empire. It is almost incredible, the number of cities and villages which, according to Josephus, it contained. They hung on the sides of the mountains, stretching downward to the shore of the Lake below, so that Christ, sitting on this mount, seemed to have the world at his feet ; and to be speaking, not to his disciples only, but to all mankind. /

"And he opened his mouth and taught them." The first thing which strikes us is the absence of pretension. There is no air of assumption, either in attitude or look or voice. He does not stand erect, like an orator, but takes his seat on the ground, after the Oriental custom. He does not even raise his hand to hush the impatient crowd : it does not need to be stilled ; for as it creeps closer to his feet, it hushes itself, that it may catch every word. He gathers his little family around him, for his words are to them, though heard by the multitude that presses forward to be within sound of his voice. They listen for the first sentence. And what is it? Some great swelling word of philosophy? Some abstract definition or subtle analysis? Nothing of all this, but simply "Blessed are the poor in spirit, for theirs is the kingdom of heaven." The first word of the Sermon on the Mount is a word of consolation. The world is full of suffering, which Christ comes to relieve. In the multitude that gathered round him, as in the population of Galilee, the mass were poor, and it may be that he had first in mind the literal poor, towards whom his heart was full of tenderness, and in reversing the maxims of the world, he shows how the poor may be rich, and those who have little to look for in this world may be heirs of the kingdom of heaven.

But the poor are not the only ones who need to be told where true peace is to be found. The world is all astray, seeking happiness where it can find only disappointment. There is a philosophy of the world, embodied in its maxims —a philosophy in proverbs—which sums up its average wisdom. It is a philosophy which glorifies success ; which counts him the happy man who has had his fill of gratified avarice and ambition. We are all more or less under this illusion. If we were asked to point out the most happy men within the circle of our observation, we might point to the most successful, to the rich, the great, and the proud.

Not so speaks our Master. His philosophy is directly opposed to that of the world. It is not in gratifying the passions, but in subduing them, that rest is to be found. Blessed—not are the rich, but the poor ; not the proud, but the meek ; not they that rejoice, but they that mourn.

Does it seem as if these things were spoken by way of paradox, merely to startle and surprise? But that was not the way of our Master, who never said anything for effect, but spoke always in the severe simplicity of truth. We have to learn by bitter experience that it is the only truth. Let the philosopher take these maxims of Christ, and sub-

ject them to the most rigorous analysis, and he will find
them to contain not the truth in a metaphor, but the truth
in its most literal sense.   Can any statement be more pre-
cisely true than that there is more of peace in a lowly
spirit than in a proud spirit?   Pride is an uneasy and
uncomfortable temper, always restless and dissatisfied.
Humility alone can give peace, because it alone is consist-
ent with our real condition.   If a man thinks highly of
himself, he thinks falsely.   Whatever may be our position
as related to others, yet in the eye of God, who alone sees
things as they are, we are but creatures of a moment,
" whose foundation is in the dust, which are crushed before
the moth " :

> " O why should the spirit of mortal be proud ? "

When a man is content to take the place in his own esteem
that he has in the eye of God, then he will find that perfect
repose and tranquillity of mind which is the first condition
of true peace and happiness.

"Ye are the light of the world!"   This was spoken to
his disciples, not to inflame their pride, but to give them a
new sense of obligation.   Looking up from the spot where
our Saviour sat, we can see even now a town on the crest
of a mountain (Safed), the very same which, it is believed,
caught his eye at the moment, and gave emphasis to his
illustration : "A city that is set on a hill cannot be hid."
So luminous should be the power of example.   It was not
enough to have a secret desire for goodness : "Let your
light so shine before men that they may see your good
works, and glorify your Father which is in heaven."

Then declaring that he is not come to destroy the law
or the prophets, but to fulfil them, Christ gives them a
broader meaning by extending the obligation to the heart.
Lust is adultery, and hatred is murder.   No form of devo-

tion can make up for inward bitterness : "If thou bring
thy gift to the altar, and there rememberest that thy
brother hath aught against thee, leave there thy gift before
the altar, and go thy way ; first be reconciled to thy
brother, and then come and offer thy gift." He abrogates
the law of revenge—the *lex talionis :* "An eye for an eye,
and a tooth for a tooth " ; "I say unto you, Love your
enemies ; bless them that curse you ; do good to them
that hate you ; pray for them which despitefully use you
and persecute you." This is a revolution in morals! In
presenting a standard of virtue so exalted, our Lord en-
forces it by the highest of all examples : "That ye may be
the children of your Father which is in heaven : for he
maketh his sun to rise on the evil and on the good, and
his rain to descend on the just and on the unjust. Be ye
therefore perfect even as your Father in heaven is perfect."
Here virtue soars to the highest point. Compared with
this, what is ordinary virtue ? Patriotism is only selfishness in an enlarged form, an inseparable part of which is
"Thou shalt love thy neighbor and hate thine enemy."
But here man is taught to cultivate a love which is that of
God himself. /

So of the religious offices of almsgiving and prayer.
Christ counts for little the ostentatious and boastful parade
of charity : but the secret offering, unseen by all but God,
which falls like the dew upon some blighted and suffering
human life—that alone has any virtue in his sight. And
prayer! How vain and idle are the long petitions which
resound in public places, to attract the ear of the multitude! "After this manner pray : 'Our Father.'" That
word changes at once the relation of man to his Maker.
It is not a cold and distant Power, enthroned among the
stars, to which man offers a worship born of fear rather
than of love, but a Being with whom he may claim kindred,

to whom he stands in the nearest relation, and may approach with the tenderest words. "*Our* Father"—not mine only, but the God and Father of all mankind ; and yet mine, in the sense that he is very near to me, as to every human soul. With such a Father, how sweet it is to be a child! "Heaven," it is said, "is about us in our infancy." But what is the heaven of poetry to the heaven of love ? In our Father's house we are at home ; we hide in his pavilion ; we are folded under the shadow of his wings ; and in the warmth of that Infinite Heart our trembling hearts cease their throbbings and are still. "Hallowed be thy name : Thy kingdom come : Thy will be done on earth as it is in heaven." Short sentences, few words, but with a sweep that includes the universe. He who bows upon his knees with every morning's light, and repeats these words from the bottom of his heart—who can say lovingly "Our Father," and reverently "Hallowed be thy name : Thy kingdom come," and submissively (though it be sometimes with a breaking heart) "THY WILL BE DONE ! "—we had almost said, need offer no other prayer. At least he has caught the spirit of all true devotion. For ourselves, our wants are few : daily bread ; forgiveness, (which is promised to us only as we forgive those who have trespassed against us,) and freedom from temptation and from sin—this is all for which we need to pray— these are all the real wants which we have occasion to bring to the Giver of all good.

To minds troubled with care and longing for worldly possessions, what a rebuke is this : "Lay not up treasures upon earth, but lay up treasures in heaven! " Vain are the anxieties with which men vex themselves in all the years through which they make their journey to the grave. "Take no thought for your life what ye shall eat, or what ye shall drink, or what ye shall put on." At that moment,

it may be, birds, which abound in Palestine, were flying
across the sky, and instantly he takes a lesson from them :
"Behold the fowls of the air ! they sow not, neither do
they reap, nor gather into barns ; yet your Heavenly
Father feedeth them." Another glance takes in the wild
flowers that cover the valleys and the hills, and he adds
"And why take ye thought for raiment? Consider the
lilies of the field, how they grow ; they toil not, neither do
they spin. And yet Solomon in all his glory was not
arrayed like one of these."

He cautions his disciples against that hasty judgment
of others, to which we are all so much inclined, disposing
lightly and flippantly of reputations which are dear to
them as ours are to ourselves. What if the same easy
and careless mode of judgment were turned upon us!
How could our characters stand the scrutiny? Might we
not find, at the very moment we were endeavoring to
pluck a mote out of our neighbor's eye, that we had a
beam in our own? In repressing this proneness to harsh
judgment, our Lord lays his finger on one of the chief
vices of society, one which was the reproach of ancient
times as it is the scandal of our own. Nothing in all the
wide round of human wickedness is more selfish or cruel
than this mean and malignant depreciation of our neighbors, as if we were better than they. In this as in all
things—in words or in deeds—there is one rule to be followed : " Whatsoever ye would that men should do unto
you, do ye even so unto them "—a rule so simple and so
comprehensive that all the ages have pronounced it the
Golden Rule, as summing up the whole duty of men in
their relations to each other. /

Last of all, our Master enjoins a transparent sincerity.
Vain is concealment or hypocrisy. "By their fruits ye
shall know them." Truth alone is the foundation of char-

acter, and that only will stand when all else is swept away. It is vain to build upon the sand, however imposing may be the structure to the eye. "And the rain descended, and the floods came, and the winds blew and beat upon that house, and it fell, and great was the fall of it." /

Absorbed in such thoughts, we lingered on the Mount of the Beatitudes, as if chained by a spell which we would not have broken. Were such words ever uttered by human lips before? Was there ever such wisdom united with such charity? The scene on the Mount is indeed changed ; the multitude is departed, and the Great Teacher ; but the words here spoken have gone into all the world ; they have been translated into all the languages of men, and are as fresh to-day as eighteen hundred years ago. They cannot die. As long as there are human hearts to suffer—men to sorrow and to weep— they will come to Christ the Consoler. Compared with this, what is the wisdom of the world! The sayings of all the philosophers—not only of the Grecian sages, but of those who assumed the lofty role of founders of Religion, of Mohammed, of Confucius, and of Buddha—would not make the Sermon on the Mount. Its superiority to their teachings strikes even those who are accounted unbelievers, who cannot but recognize this sublime morality, and pay their tribute to him who gave it to the world. Says the celebrated French writer, Rousseau : /

I confess that the majesty of the Scriptures astonishes me; the sanctity of the Gospel speaks to my heart. See the books of the philosophers with all their pomp—how small are they compared to this! Can it be that a book at once so sublime and so simple should be the work of men ? Can it be that he whose history it gives should be only a man himself ? Is there here the tone of an enthusiast, of an ambitious sectary ? What mildness, what purity in his manners ! What touching grace in his instructions ! What elevation in his maxims ! What profound wisdom

in his discourses! What presence of mind, what finesse and yet
what justice in his answers! What empire over his passions!
Where is the man, where is the sage, who knows how to act, to
suffer, and to die, without weakness and without ostentation?
When Plato painted his ideal just man, covered with all the op-
probrium of crime, while worthy of all the rewards of virtue, he
drew trait for trait the picture of Jesus Christ: the resemblance is
so striking that all the Fathers perceived it, and it is impossible
to mistake it. What prejudice, what blindness, to dare to com-
pare the son of Sophronisca with the son of Mary! What a
distance from the one to the other! Socrates dying without pain,
without ignominy, sustains easily his character to the end; and if
this calm death had not honored his life, one might have doubted
whether Socrates with all his genius was more than a sophist.
He discovered, they tell us, the principles of morality; but others
before him had put them in practice; he only put in words what
they had done; he but turned their examples into lessons. Aris-
tides had been just before Socrates had set forth the nature of
justice; Leonidas had died for his country before Socrates had
made it a duty to love one's country. Sparta was sober before
Socrates praised sobriety; before he defined virtue, Greece
abounded in virtuous men. But where did Jesus find among
his own people that pure and elevated morality of which he gave
at once the lessons and the example? From the bosom of the
most furious fanaticism was heard the highest wisdom, and the
simplicity of the most heroic virtues honored the vilest of all
peoples. The death of Socrates, philosophizing tranquilly with
his friends, is the mildest that one could desire: that of Jesus
expiring in torments, injured, railed at, cursed by a whole people,
is the most horrible that one could dread. Socrates, taking the
poisoned cup, thanks him who presents it and who weeps: Jesus
in the midst of frightful sufferings, prays for his enraged murderers. Truly, if the life and the death of Socrates were those of
a philosopher, the life and the death of Jesus Christ were those of
a God! /

Yes truly : " the life and the death of Jesus Christ were
those of a God "! No other explanation will meet the
case. Natural causes utterly fail to account for the stu-
pendous reality. And so the teachings of the Great Master

are far beyond the range of human wisdom or philosophy. Genius can do many things, but in the Sermon on the Mount there is that which is not genius—it is Divinity.*

After this long musing on the Mount of the Beatitudes, we rode on silently. In the presence of such a scene, one cannot easily descend to the level of historical associations, however great. Had we place for anything else, we might remember that on this very mount, and on the plain around it, was fought nearly seven hundred years ago (July 5th, 1187) the last battle of the Crusaders, whom Saladin here crushed by one tremendous blow ; and yet the contrast of such terrible scenes does but heighten the sacred beauty of this spot—the Mount of Peace rising above the Sea of Blood. /

In turning away from the Mount of the Beatitudes, we were not leaving the scenes of our Lord's ministry : for before us, in the deep bosom of the hills, was the Sea of Galilee. The descent is not unlike that to the Dead Sea. The hills indeed are not so bleak as those of the Wilderness of Judea, nor is the depression of the waters so great ; but looking down from the heights above, it seemed as if we were going down to the bottom of the mountains.

* The force of this testimony was felt by no one more than the late Daniel Webster, who, on his death-bed, on a Sabbath evening, Oct. 10th, 1852, (he died on the 24th) dictated, and on the 15th "revised and corrected with his own hand," this inscription to be placed on his tomb :

"LORD, I BELIEVE ; HELP THOU MINE UNBELIEF.

"Philosophical argument, especially that drawn from the vastness of the universe, in comparison with the apparent insignificance of this globe, has sometimes shaken my reason for the faith which is in me ; but my heart has always assured and reassured me that the Gospel of Jesus Christ must be a Divine Reality. The Sermon on the Mount cannot be a mere human production. This belief enters into the very depth of my conscience. The whole history of man proves it."/

Below us in full view, on the shores of the Lake, was a town of some pretensions as towns go in Palestine. Seen from a distance, with its ancient tower and its encircling wall, it appears not unworthy of a history that dates from the time of the Romans, and of its Imperial name of Tiberias. But as we draw nearer, its grandeur disappears, its tower cannot boast of being a fortress, and there are sad rents in its battered wall. Riding through its ancient archway, and along its narrow streets, we observe at once a striking contrast with Nazareth, which has a Christian, while Tiberias has a Jewish, population. At almost every door and in almost every shop we recognized the corkscrew curls and the peculiar dress, the cap of fur and the long gabardine, which in all the East mark the sons of Abraham. /

Passing through the town to the farther end, we found our tents pitched on the shore of the lake, and were never more glad to get into camp. Not only had we taken a long day's ride, but in descending the hills we had come into a warmer region. Owing to its depression, the Sea of Galilee, like the Dead Sea, has a tropical climate, so that we were heated as well as fatigued when we crawled off our horses. Hardly had we dismounted before I strolled down the lake to seek a retired place to bathe. There are hot sulphur baths close to the shore, which have been famous for two thousand years, to which Herod came to cleanse his blood. The springs still come steaming out of the hills, and are the resort of multitudes. A large building encloses a circular bathing-room, where at any hour of the day may be found many plunging into the water, or sitting on the marble rim of the basin sweltering in the hot vapor : but as it seemed to be a sort of Pool of Bethesda for those suffering from all kinds of diseases, I was content with mere observation, and sought rather the

cool margin of the lake, and was soon swimming in its
tranquil waters. /

Thus refreshed, I returned to sit in the tent door in
the cool of the day, and watch the shadows creeping over
"the deep," and climbing the sides of the opposing hills.
The waters were calm and still, the evening wind causing
only the gentlest ripple on the bosom of the lake. "The
shades of night were gathering fast"; but remembering
who once walked upon these waters, I could not doubt that
his form was still gliding through the shadows; there were
soft whisperings in the air, and patient, gentle words of
forgiveness; and to the trembling heart came the reassur-
ing voice : "It is I : be not afraid ! "/

# CHAPTER XIV.

## ROUND THE SEA OF GALILEE.

It is not a sea, but a lake, and not even a lake of broad expanse, as we measure lakes in America, but rather resembles one of the small but exquisitely beautiful English lakes, like Windermere, or a Scotch loch lying in the lap of the Grampian Hills. It is larger than Loch Katrine, but smaller than Loch Lomond, and much inferior in the majesty given to it by a girdle of lofty mountains. In this respect it is not even the first in Palestine : for it is much inferior to the Dead Sea, both in size and in the boldness of the surrounding scenery. The encircling hills do not rise so high, nor descend so abruptly. The slopes are more gentle. Instead of coming down sheer into the lake, there is an interval between the waters and the hills. As I stand upon the shore this morning, the hills on the other side are indeed beautiful as the sun rises over them ; but they have not the sombre grandeur of the mountains of Moab, which at this hour cast dark shadows on the waters below. Perhaps we might distinguish the two bodies of water by saying that while one has a character of majesty, the other has that of softness and grace—fit symbols of the histories they tell, the one of wrath and ruin, of judgment and destruction ; the other of mildness and mercy, of gentleness and peace./

But whatever of majesty may be wanting in the Galilean lake, is more than made up by its sacred associations : for it is the Lake of Jesus, as it was the chief scene of his ministry. Here he lived for the greater part of three years. He walked along this pebbled beach ; he sailed across these waters, or sat in a boat and talked to the multitude on the shore ; and at night retired into the recesses of these hills to pray : so that everything around us—the hills and waters, the waving trees, and even the moaning night winds—all speak of him. With such associations, it is not too much to say with Dean Stanley that this is " the most sacred sheet of water that this earth contains."/

But why did our Lord choose a lake for the scene of his ministry, and not only the lake-side, but the lake itself ? If we were to follow the method of those naturalistic writers, who are ready with a plausible explanation of everything, we might suppose that he was attracted to the spot by his love of nature. Renan, who has made such a careful study of the life of Jesus in its merely human aspect, and in its relation to its surroundings of place and time, remarks constantly this exquisite sensibility (which he would perhaps say was a poetic temperament) to the beauty of the external world. Christ loved the fields and the flowers, the mountain top with its wide horizon, and the soft, tender beauty of the valley below. We can well believe that he was keenly alive to the natural beauty of this lake, while it was to him also a mirror of human life—its changing moods of storm and calm, emblems of the agitations of the human soul, which would subside only when he should say : Peace, be still !/

Other reasons occur to us. In coming to the Lake of Galilee, our Lord did not wander far away from home. It was but a day's journey from Nazareth, where he had passed the long period from childhood to mature manhood. As he had just entered on his active ministry, he naturally sought the centres of population. The province of Galilee had at this time about three millions of inhabitants. The hills around the lake were thick with villages, and swarming with people. Travellers in Italy are struck with the dense population of some of the mountain districts, where innumerable hamlets are scattered among the orange and the lemon groves, and cling, like trailing vines, to the sides of the hills. Not unlike this were the hillsides round the Sea of Galilee, while its shores were lined with fishing villages. Then, as now, the lake abounded with fish, which supplied food for a large population. The lake was alive with boats, not only in the daytime, but at night, when the stars shine so brightly in these Eastern heavens ; and if the Hebrews were a musical people, it is not unreasonable to suppose that often the boatmen sang their native airs, which echoed from shore to shore, as the waters of Venice echo with the song of the gondolier. /

Access to these multitudes was rendered easy by the climate, as well as by the country. The ministry of our Lord was an itinerant ministry. He had no fixed place of teaching. He did not set up a school of theology, like Hillel or other learned rabbis ; nor did he preach chiefly in the synagogues, but out of doors, under the open sky. He went from city to city and village to village. This wandering life could be possible only in a mild climate. Such is that of the Sea of Galilee. Owing to its great depression, it has a southern climate in a northern latitude. Its vegetation is tropical : palms grow in the open air. Hence the people lived out of doors, as the people now live round the Bay of Naples, and could come together at any place or any hour, when the Great Teacher appeared.

Thus wandering along the lake shore, he fixed his eye upon the Twelve. Can any one suppose it a mere chance, or a matter of indifference, that he chose his first disciples from among fishermen? All over the world a seafaring population has a peculiar character—open, frank, and manly. Men of the sea have to do with a restless and treacherous element, and frequent exposure to danger makes them fearless and bold. Of such men of the sea did Christ choose those who were to follow him, whom he would make fishers of men.

Here was a little world by itself, shut in by the hills, yet full of life, to which the Master came. But life was not all that he needed : at times he needed a separation from life, absolute and complete. By such separation the great religious spirits of the world have nursed their strength. An irresistible impulse leads them to seek the wilderness. So Jesus loved silence and solitude. He did not shun the society of men so long as he could do them good. But when the work of the day was done, he sought retirement. At Jerusalem he found it near at hand on the Mount of Olives. Here he found it on the lake, or the hills around it. Thus he had the busy world on one side, and perfect seclusion on the other. He could preach all day to the multitude that thronged him ; he could heal the sick, and labor to the point of weariness and exhaustion ; and then could put off from the shore into the lake, and float in the twilight, or seek the recesses of the hills, and there continue all night in prayer to God.

And now we were standing on the shore of this Sea of Galilee, full of such sacred memories. To see it well, the traveller may choose either of two ways—to ride around it or to sail over it. We preferred the latter. The facilities are not great. On this whole lake, once alive with its fisheries, there are now less than a dozen boats. Fortunately one of these was lying on the beach, which we engaged for the day, with its native crew. It was probably the same kind of boat or "ship" used in the time of our Saviour, with which he often crossed these waters. It had half a dozen boatmen, which we found few enough: for although there was, a light wind, which just filled the single sail, and steadied the boat, we had to rely mainly on their oars, which were long, heavy, and clumsy, being only small trees, with the "butt end" hewn down to make a narrow blade. Spreading our tent blankets on the seats or in the bottom of the boat, we sat or crouched as we could, while the men edged in between us wherever they could get a sweep for their arms.

The distance from Tiberias to the head of the lake is eight or nine miles, which, with the Italian boatmen on Lake Como or in Venice, would not seem very much ; but the boats here are not made for speed—they are rather fishermen's boats, with broad bottoms to take in a good haul of the net. |

But who would hasten his speed along these sacred shores? The morning was not made for haste, but for floating in dreamy and delicious reveries. It had been very hot on shore, but the heat was soon tempered by the lake breeze. In the novel scene each one showed his bent. Weeden, as if he were on a sailing excursion at home, began to hum "'Way down on Bingo Farm"; while Mrs. Adams, entering more into the spirit of the scene, sang softly to herself "Fierce was the wild billow." I had my eye fixed on the shores as we glided by. Tiberias is far more picturesque from the water than from the land. On the other side of the lake, to which we come nearer as we "launch out into the deep," is the country of the

Gadarenes. On yonder sloping hillside it is supposed the
demons entered into the swine, who, maddened with the
diabolical possession, rushed down the steep and plunged
into the sea. Northeasterly is the plain on which Christ
fed the five thousand ; and westward, where the lake
broadens out to its greatest width, is the Plain of Gennesareth, on the border of which is a miserable hamlet,
which would not have a name but for the touching story
of an unhappy woman, who brought her sorrows and her
sins to the Saviour's feet, and there found pardon and
peace. It is Magdala, which gives name to Mary Magdalene. /

While thus gazing at the shores, we were making
progress but slowly, and with both sail and oars it took us
four hours to come to the upper end of the lake, where the
hills part to the right and the left, opening a broad plain
through which the Jordan descends to the sea. As the
forenoon was nearly spent, we were looking out for a place
for our noonday camp. Our dragoman pointed to a tree
on the shore which, standing quite solitary, presented the
only hope of shade. A tree is a great thing under a
Syrian sun. We congratulated ourselves on the prospect,
and were already beginning to feel its coolness in anticipation, when we descried in the distance a party on horseback, which had made the journey round the head of the
lake, and were now coming over the hills, evidently bent
on the same destination. They discovered us at the
moment that we discovered them, and put spurs to their
horses to be first on the ground. It was a race between
horses and boatmen. Had the distances been the same,
we should have had no chance at all ; but as we were perhaps a mile nearer the landing, we determined to make the
most of it, and starting up from our seats, we cheered our
men with hope of reward. Backsheesh always has a mirac-

ulous effect on the spirit of a Syrian, and the six swarthy
backs bent to their oars and pulled as if for life, and suddenly the battered boat (like an old horse that has been
jogging along the road, till a sudden cut of the whip wakes
him up and sets him flying) began to kick up her heels,
and to rush madly through the water. In a few minutes
she struck the beach, and leaping from the bow, we rushed
for the tree, and spread our rugs at its foot, which was as
good as hoisting a flag to take possession of a conquered
country. The ground was ours, and we "squatted" on it
with a proud sense of possession. Hardly were we seated
when the mounted party came up at full speed. It proved
to be not wholly a party of strangers, as it was composed
of English officers, some of whom I had met in Jerusalem.
They were attached to the Bacchante, which had been taking the young Princes round the world, and was now
sailing slowly along the Syrian coast, while they, under the
guidance of their tutors, were making visits to different
parts of Palestine. As the ship was at Acre, this party had
taken advantage of being in port for a day or two, to ride
over the hills and visit the Sea of Galilee. The dragoman
was a Syrian from Beirut, a former pupil of Dr. Post,
whom we had met in Cairo, and who, as the party rode up,
recognized me, and shouted my name. Thus hailed, an
American is expected "not to be backward in coming
forward," and I responded warmly, inviting them to join
our camp, an invitation which they soon accepted. But
for the moment they were in full rush, and dashed away
like wild Indians, and did not draw rein till they had
reached the banks of the Jordan. Here they sat on their
horses, all aglow with the excitement of their ride, firing
guns, as a sort of naval salute to "Old Jordan," which,
descending from its birthplace among the northern hills,
here melts into the sea. Having thus let off a little of their

superfluous spirits, they jogged back slowly, and joined
our camp, and we spent a pleasant hour or two together.
While sitting here, we had an unexpected sight, in a great
company of Bedaween, with two hundred camels, which
they had been pasturing among the hills and valleys of
Galilee, who were now returning across the Jordan to their
own country in the land of Bashan. I had seen nothing
like it since we left the desert. On they came, big camels
and little camels, with Arabs mounted and on foot, altogether a host of Midianites. Seeing us under the tree,
they stopped for a brief parley, and were much amazed
when the Commander of the Bacchante took up his breech-
loader, and putting in the cartridges, loaded and fired in
an instant. The Commander we found very agreeable
company. The elder Prince is a sort of aid to him,
though perhaps an aid chiefly by courtesy. English
officers are generally men of great intelligence, especially
when, as in this case, they have been for a couple of years
floating about in all parts of the world, with the best
possible opportunities for obtaining information. Our
acquaintances proved most agreeable gentlemen, and I am
sure it would be a pleasure to any of our party to meet
again, on either side of the ocean, the officers whom we
met that day on the shore of the Sea of Galilee. /

After our long "nooning," they mounted to depart,
while we entered into "the ship," and were rowed a mile
or so to the eastward, to the mouth of the Jordan, before
we turned westward to Chorazin, Bethsaida, and Capernaum. The Jordan, where it empties into the lake, is a
large stream, flowing with a current almost as strong as
that at the Dead Sea. We leaped ashore, and gathered
each a handful of the minute shells which are here strown
like sand upon the beach. Hardly were we in the boat
again before a strong head-wind arose, against which it

was not easy to force our way.  The men rowed hard, but
progress was slow and difficult.  To make it worse, the
Bedaween who had passed us with their camels had stopped to take a swim in the lake; and now, seeing our
extremity, they turned towards us, at first only a few, but
soon after a much larger number, and made a sudden dash
for the boat, intending to seize hold of it, and perhaps to
climb into it, at any rate not to let go till they were bought
off.  The rascals thought they had " a sure thing," for that
the ladies would be so terrified that we would pay anything
to be rid of them.  So we might have done had we not had
a determined dragoman; but as they were nearing us,
Floyd started up with fury in his eye, and anger in his
voice, and said if they dared to come near the boat, he
would shoot every man of them as he would shoot a dog!
At this the villains turned and swam back to the shore.\

Thus we were saved from one danger, but still we made
little headway, for the wind was contrary.  Twice the boatmen cast out the anchor, and said they would not go any
further.  I am afraid they were treacherous: for this would
have compelled us to go on shore, and walk for several
miles to our camp, presenting a tempting object to the
Bedaween, who were still watching us with hungry eyes.
When they were in the water, without their guns (for many
of them carried guns), they could do nothing ; but had we
set foot on land, we should have been helplessly in their
power.  Floyd saw the danger, and once more his hot temper saved us.  His imperious manner cowed the boatmen
into obedience.  After a few minutes, they sullenly lifted
the anchor, and again took to their oars.  But the wind was
too much for their strength.  At last the ladies were asked
to turn their gaze seaward or in the direction of the mountains, while a couple of the men, casting off their garments,
like Peter of old, plunged into the lake, and swam ashore /

with a rope in their hands, and getting a "belay" around
rocks, pulled with all their might, while those in the boat
rowed hard ; and so by the most fatiguing labor, we crept
slowly along.  Once we gave our men a breathing spell, as
we anchored at Tell Hum and went on shore, and wading
through the long grass, came upon broken columns lying
here and there—the ruins of a city that has passed away,
and whose very name is in dispute, some claiming that it
was Capernaum itself, while others identify it with Chorazin.
Here, as elsewhere round the upper end of the lake, ruins
and fields alike are relieved of any sombre appearance by
the masses of color thrown in by the great and luxuriant
oleanders, which at this season are covered with blossoms.
Westward a little farther, we passed the ancient Bethsaida,
but did not land, as the best which it has to show is its situation, which is seen directly from the water—a valley which,
reaching down to the shore, furnished a site for the fishing
village which was the home of Peter, Andrew, and Philip.
It is a beautiful spot—beautiful even though the village or
town itself be gone, and only a few wretched huts mark the
place where it stood.  It has a melancholy interest as being
coupled with Chorazin in the prophetic words : "Woe unto
thee, Chorazin! woe unto thee, Bethsaida! . . . It shall be
more tolerable for Tyre and Sidon at the judgment than
for you."/

Up to this point our men had been putting forth all
their strength in rowing, but soon after we passed Bethsaida, they unbent from their oars, as we came into a little
bay which was partly sheltered from the winds, where the
water was smooth, so that at last we glided gently to the
shore.  The experience of this afternoon, though more wearisome than dangerous, showed what the lake might be in
a storm, when the winds from the mountains come down
upon it and lash it into fury.  Then it becomes indeed a

place of danger, that might well have justified the terror of
the disciples, when they roused their Master from his slumber to save them from instant destruction. /

We landed at Khan Minyeh, and found our tents, which
had been sent round by land to meet us, pitched a few
rods back from the shore, near a beautiful spring which
issued from under high rocks.   Here is the traditional site
of the ancient Capernaum.   I know that its identity has
been fiercely disputed ; explorers are divided between
Khan Minyeh and Tell Hum.   In such cases, where both
sides are maintained with an array of learning, the ordinary traveller will fall back upon common report, and accept
that which has the authority of tradition.   Certainly this
was worthy to have been the site of a great city.   It is on
the borders of the Plain of Gennesareth, which furnished
ample room on which the city could expand.   It is at the
head of the lake, in a position favorable to such commerce
as there might be upon it, and at the same time to the traffic
with the interior : for it was the entrepôt of a great overland trade between Asia and Africa—between the valleys
of the Tigris and the Euphrates on the one hand, and the
valley of the Nile on the other.   Caravans of camels crossing the desert brought hither the riches of the farthest
East.   In the grand old Roman days, this was one of the
chief seats of Roman power in Palestine.   Here was the
residence of the Governor of Galilee.   The province was
traversed by Roman roads ; the city was watered by Roman aqueducts : and Roman soldiers kept guard in its
streets.   Our camp was at the foot of a cliff, on the top of
which is a small plateau, which must have been included
within the city.   Looking up to this height, it seemed
probable that there was an upper town and a lower town,
and that this elevated plateau was the Acropolis, on which
stood the Governor's Palace, and the citadel, and a temple

to the gods, or whatever might show forth the Imperial splendor. Perhaps our Lord had this literal elevation in his eye, as a type of the haughtiness and pride of the city, when he said "And thou, Capernaum, which art exalted to heaven, shalt be thrust down to hell! " This was not a curse, but a judgment—a solemn declaration by one who saw the end from the beginning, of the inevitable ruin which waits on proud and insolent wickedness. How that word has been accomplished, we see to-day. Of all that ancient magnificence, not a trace remains. One can hardly imagine how utter is the desolation. In some of these old towns around the lake not a human being is left. Here where once stood a great city, with a multitude thronging its streets, every footstep is departed. This plain was once full of busy life ; this lake was animated by boats gliding to and fro. Now there is scarcely a sail upon the water or a footprint on the shore. The night that we camped here, there was a young moon in the sky that just revealed the outlines of the hills, and gleamed faintly on the waters—one of those nights that make us listen for some "floating whisper on the hill " ; but all was silent as the grave. The only sound that we heard all night long, was that of the jackals that made their habitations in the rocks, whose mournful cry at midnight seemed to give voice to the mighty desolation. The woe had been fulfilled. /

# CHAPTER XV.

/As we broke camp in the morning, and rode up the hill, which I have supposed was the ancient Acropolis, we turned to take one more look at the Sea of Galilee lying at our feet. On the eastern side the hills were still partly in shadow, but the morning light was creeping over them, bringing into view the outline of the sacred shores. Almost every spot within the sweep of the eye was connected with the history of our Lord. Capernaum was his home for the greater part of the three years of his ministry—a period more important than the preceding thirty years, which he spent at Nazareth : for here his life was not one of obscurity, but of incessant activity ; his teaching was chiefly on these shores and waters, and now his blessed words seem to float upward from the lake below, while from the Plain of Gennesareth the air, fresh with morning dew, comes like the breath of God. In the presence of such a scene, it is almost an impertinence to speak : one is held silent and motionless. For a few moments we sat on our horses, not saying a word, and then turned and silently rode away. /

As we leave the lake behind, we enter a rough hill-country, which is the character of this portion of Galilee.

Our faces were set towards the North, following a route parallel to the course of the Jordan, although we were not in the valley, nor even within sight of it, as our view was interrupted by the hills, among which we were riding all the forenoon ; and as of course there are no roads, but only bridle-paths, we had to pick our way among the stones. The country seemed deserted of human habitations : there were no towns—we did not see even a village. Its appearance was made still more desolate by being without trees. While riding among the hills, I did not see a single tree. Whether this be owing to the government tax on trees, or to the wastefulness of the people in cutting for fuel every young tree almost as soon as it shows its head above ground, I know not : I only state the fact, that the landscape was absolutely treeless. But though in this respect it is stripped and barren as the desert, it is not like the desert in the poorness of its soil or the absence of cultivation : for rough and rocky as is this portion of Northern Galilee, it is neither uninhabited nor uncultivated. There were men ploughing in the fields, as we had seen them in the South Country when we first entered Palestine. Yet here, as there, the mode of agriculture is very poor ; the oxen are small ; the plough is of wood, with an iron point, and only a single handle, as it is guided by one hand, while the other holds an ox-goad, with which the poor little beasts are punched and prodded over the rough soil. Still with all these drawbacks, the country was fairly cultivated, some fields were waving with ripening harvests ; and the people were better-looking, they had lighter complexions and more animated features, than those we had seen before, and responded pleasantly to our salaams as we passed. Our knowledge of Arabic is not extensive, being confined to half a dozen words ; but what we lack in number, we make up in reiteration. When we see a dashing rider approaching, we sit bolt upright in our saddles, and explode "Marhaba!" at him with a sonorous voice, which at once commands his attention, and evokes from the depth of his bosom a guttural reply. We have not met anybody so churlish as not to return our salutations. Even the Bedaween are not to be outdone in politeness, although in other circumstances they might have considered it in the way of business to rob us if they could. So we jogged up hill and down dale, in a flow of spirits which made us forget the rough paths under our feet. The mules had a hard time of it, carrying their heavy loads over the hills : but they did not seem to mind it, their bells ringing merrily, in unison with the general cheerfulness. As a reward for our good nature, after a few hours the appearance of the country changed from desolateness to fertility. Towards noon we again caught the gleam of waters in the distance. Before us opened a broad and beautiful valley, through which stretched a sheet of water more like a lake than a river—indeed it was both—for we had come back to the Jordan, which here overflows its banks, and spreads out so widely that for a few miles the river is expanded into a lake. We were approaching the famous Waters of Merom, around which is a broad belt of the richest alluvial soil. This is the Plain of the Jordan, which is here nearly as wide as the Plain of Jericho, and much more highly cultivated. /

The ride of the afternoon was a pleasant contrast to that of the morning, as we came down out of the hills, and entered this broad and fertile plain. The sight of water is grateful to the eye after passing over a rugged country, and still more so when it is bordered with fertile pastures that reach back to the foot of the hills. We found the valley very populous, although its population is an uncertain and migratory one. The Plain of the Jordan is one

great pasture-ground of the Bedaween. How it comes to
be so is quite apparent from its geography. The mountains, which form a natural barrier on the lower Jordan,
here sink down so that there is nothing to keep out the
Ishmaelites, to whom no land is sacred from invasion.
They come over in vast numbers from their homes among
the hills of Bashan, bringing their flocks and herds with
them, and camp for a few months till they have eaten up
the pasturage. They live in huts, or in tents, made, as on
the desert, of the hair of the black goats—a custom inher-
ited from patriarchal times, as we read in the Bible of
"the black tents of Kedar." The cloth woven from this
material is very strong. We saw some Arabs moving their
camp, and from the number of men it took to carry one of
these tent covers, it seemed as if it must be as heavy as the
thickest canvas used for the sails of ships. Of course it is
very durable, as it must be to withstand the variations of
heat and cold, and the early and latter rains, which sometimes come down in floods. Half a dozen of these broad
tents will make an Arab village; and when pitched, as
they often are, on the sides of the hills, they are very picturesque. The Plain of the Jordan gave us the most
pleasant side of Arab life that we saw anywhere. The
people are engaged in peaceful occupations; they are
shepherds, and there is always something poetical in a
pastoral life. A shepherd tending his flock of sheep is a
pleasing figure in a landscape; even the buffaloes wallowing in the shallow waters, among the reeds and rushes,
attract the eye as a picture of lazy life, which transports
one's thoughts to the interior of Africa. Our road, while
leading through the plain, yet kept at a distance from
the water, as the nearer ground is often wet and marshy;
and as we rode along under the shadow of the hills,
several times this afternoon, we heard a shepherd's boy /

playing on a reed pipe, to call his sheep. With this pastoral music in our ears, we pitched our tents on the bank of one of the tributary streams of the Jordan, in full view of Mount Hermon. Never did tired travellers camp in a lovelier spot. We had had a long and weary day's march, and the rest was very grateful. The people gathered about us with curiosity to see the strangers, but not in an unfriendly way; though Floyd cautioned us not to let them presume on any familiarity, saying rather brusquely "If we make friends with them, they will swarm down upon us and clean us out." We observed that, mild-mannered as they seemed, they all carried long-handled spears, which might come into instant use on a very slight provocation. But as long as they let us alone, and kept at a safe distance, we could look on and see how they enjoyed themselves, with no uncomfortable drawbacks. It was pleasant to see them light-hearted and happy; and when, in the morning, just before we mounted our horses, the men and women of an Arab camp formed a ring on the green sward, and executed a rustic dance before setting out for the flocks which they were to watch through the day, it was a sight to make a traveller think he had suddenly lighted on a scene in Arcadia. In these outdoor exhibitions Arab life is seen at its best. One must not penetrate too far into the interior. The villages are *not* Arcadian. As we resumed our march, and after a long ride up the Plain of the Jordan, passed round the head of the Waters of Merom, our route led through a village of huts made of a kind of matting woven of the reeds which grow on the borders of the lake, and hung on cross poles, not unlike those I had seen in India and Burmah. They were wretched habitations, but swarming with life. It was plain that there was no danger of the race dying out. As we rode through the long, narrow path between these miserable dwellings, men, women, and children rushed to the doors to see us pass. Every little hand was stretched out for something. "Backsheesh! backsheesh!" was the cry; and as if even this were too much for children's throats, the word was shortened into "'sheesh," which was hissed from hundreds of little voices. It seemed as if the very dogs yelped backsheesh. /

When we turned away from the Waters of Merom, we had "passed over Jordan," and were in the enemy's country, or what might have been so had we been near the Dead Sea. But though we had crossed the river, we were still among its springs, which we were following up to their source in the sides of Hermon. The country gradually ascends, leading us upward. Part of our way we followed the track of an old Roman road, and crossed one of the principal affluents of the Jordan by a bridge whose massive arch still shows the work of Roman hands. Wherever we come upon the footsteps of these ancient masters of the world, they are marked by roads and bridges—the signs of their civilization and the instruments of their power. "All roads lead to Rome." So it was meant to be, not only in Italy and Gaul and Spain, but even in remote provinces, where easy means of communication drew towards Rome the most distant parts of the mighty empire. Continuing our course, we came to Dan, the spot to which Abraham pursued the Amorites who had captured Lot. This is the limit of the Land of Canaan, which is defined as reaching "from Dan to Beersheba." Its northern boundary was not a mountain, but a river, or rather a fountain—the chief of the headsprings of the Jordan. Here we came upon a scene as pleasing as it was unexpected—a party of natives returning from Tiberias, where they had been to bathe in the hot springs. They were all in gay attire, like Italian or Spanish peas-

ants decked out for a *festa*.  A pretty company of pilgrims
truly!  The bright-eyed Syrian girls were in their "Sunday's best," and resting under some large oaks which
shaded the fountain.  So charming was the picture they
made in their gay dresses, sitting under the trees, that we
felt almost guilty to disturb them, though the bridle-path
led through the group ; but we made the best apology we
could, by touching our caps and bowing very low, as we
rode through the stream, and up the bank, and under the
oaks.  It was a pleasant relief to the squalid misery of
which one sees so much in Palestine, to come upon such a
scene of innocent festivity. /

Another hour's ride brought us to Banias, where we
halted at noon, not in a clump of trees, but in a large and
stately grove, the very air of which was made musical by
the sound of streams, which were bubbling and dashing
around us.  It reminded me a little of Tivoli, though the
waters do not pour from any "headlong height," but rush
upward from the bowels of the earth.  Here is another
source of the Jordan, which issues from a cave, as the
Ganges flows out from under a glacier of the Himalayas.
These sparkling blue waters look as if they came out of a
region of icy cold.  The spot is one of great natural
beauty, with its mingled woods and rocks and streams.
In the days of the old mythology, such nooks and dells
were haunted.  There were sylvan and woodland deities—
gods of the woods and streams ; and we are not surprised
to find the cliffs above this fountain of the Jordan carved
into shrines. /

Banias is also a place of historical interest, from the
many traces which it has of Roman occupation.  Situated
at the head of the Jordan valley, it marks a natural divis-
ion of the country.  Here we leave Palestine and enter
Syria.  Its position also, at the foot of Mount Hermon,

which of itself forms the strongest defence in its rear, is a military one, as it holds the key to the province of Galilee. Accordingly it was fortified by the Romans, and a town rose on this spot which, in honor of the Emperor and of the Governor, received the double name of Cæsarea-Philippi. All this region bears marks of the Roman rule. Scattered along the road from Dan to Banias, on every commanding point, are blocks of stone carefully dressed, and some of them even carved, the work of Roman hands. What remain and are above ground, are probably not a hundredth part of what lie buried in the earth, or what have been dug up and carried away : for these ruins have been the spoil of sixty generations. To this day the people use them for building. Even as we passed, we saw a party digging up the stones and carrying them off on camels. This seems almost like sacrilege, but can we blame the poor inhabitants of this region, when even the Coliseum of Rome has been despoiled to build its modern palaces ?

Cæsarea-Philippi is also an important site in the Gospel history : for it is the most northern point visited by our Lord. Here he spent six months in the last year of his ministry. Not far from this spot, some lower shoulder of Hermon is supposed to be the Mount which was the scene of the Transfiguration. /

After resting a couple of hours in the grove at Banias, we mounted and took our way through the village, where one may see here and there fallen columns, and the ruins of old Roman arches ; and then began to climb the hills, which at first were covered with olive orchards, but soon grew more bleak and bare. On the top of one is a ruined castle, whose enormous size and strength reminded me of the Castle of Heidelberg, although it is of vastly greater antiquity than any castle on the Rhine or the Neckar, the mode of dressing its stones showing that its massive foundations were laid by the Phœnicians. It commands one of the most extensive views in Palestine. These mountain fortresses are a striking feature of the country. While looking with amazement at these mighty walls, we turned westward, and saw in the distance another castle, which seemed to be the counterpart of this, although of more recent date : for it is the Chateau Neuf of the Crusaders, standing on the crest of a mountain, relieved against the glowing western sky. That mountain, like Marathon, "looks on the sea," and its castle frowns on Tyre and Sidon and the Mediterranean coast. Thus are two periods of history and two civilizations—distant not only from us, but from each other—brought " eye to eye," as Phœnicians and Crusaders signal to each other from mountain top to mountain top, across an abyss not only of centuries, but of millenniums. /

We were now on the side of the lordly Hermon, and went slowly climbing upward into the higher altitudes and the sharper air. The evening found us at an elevation of some thousands of feet. The change of temperature was very great from that of the Jordan valley, where only last night we found it extremely warm, while here to-night it is bitter cold. We are camped in a little mountain valley, which might easily be imagined to be among the Alps. It is a cheerless spot : there is not a tree in sight ; only dreary rocks, and patches of snow are still lying on the heights around us. And yet it is not without its pleasing features, in the flocks of sheep in the mountain pastures. Near us is a little Alpine village, nestled in the side of the mountain, under which it seems to be seeking shelter. The houses furnish a better protection than the tents of the Bedaween, or even their mat-covered huts. They have to be of a different material, to be habitable : for in Winter these mountain valleys are buried deep in snow. Though plain and of but one story, the houses are of stone, and being backed against the mountain, which shelters them from the winds, they may be kept at a temperature at which life can be preserved. The people are Druses—a Moslem sect chiefly known to the world by their war with the Maronites in 1860, in which they committed frightful massacres. Notwithstanding their reputation, we found them very decent-looking mountaineers. They thronged around our tents to sell eggs and chickens, and appeared quite friendly, but we did not think it wise on that account to intermit our customary precaution of sending to the sheikh for a guard. Thus in our guarded tents, wrapping our coverlids and garments about us to keep out the mountain winds, we lay down to tranquil slumber.

But a keen and frosty air is a wonderful quickener of life at the breaking of the day. Travellers must needs stir about to set the blood tingling in their veins. And so, with all the picturesqueness of its scenery, we were not unwilling to leave our Alpine home. We were early in the saddle, making long strides down the mountain. Again we had hills upon hills, and rocks upon rocks, among which crags of basalt began to crop out of the limestone, over which we plodded on patiently as we could, when suddenly, in the twinkling of an eye, there burst upon us a vision of Paradise. We had been toiling along the mountain side, when a point of the road brought us in sight of a region of boundless fertility. We were looking down upon the great Plain of Damascus, beyond which rose on the eastern horizon the black basaltic hills and mountains of the Hauran. As if to make the contrast more complete, an hour or two later, as we swept round the mountain, there rose on our left, above intervening summits which had hid his face, the snowy head of Hermon, not standing alone, but the highest peak in the long range of the Anti-Lebanon. Thus one glance took in the region of eternal snow and the region of sunshine and flowers. /

But it is one thing to have a vision of Paradise, and another to enter into it. It was a long and weary ride down the mountain. The winds from the heights above us were cold and chill, and made us shrink and shiver on our horses ; nor could we quite forget the piercing blast, even when late in the afternoon we caught sight of the great Mosque of Damascus. At last, at six o'clock, we reached the place for our camp, a little outside of the town of Katana, beside a clear rushing stream, a branch of the Pharpar. Here, though within four hours of Damascus, we pitched our tents, not only for the night, but for the following day : for once more the Sabbath had come. How delicious is it for tired pilgrims to awake one morning in the week, and not be obliged to move! To lie and think of fatigues and perils all past, with no sense of fatigue or peril near, is one of the exquisite pleasures of the traveller. Our men were long in "coming to." At last they rubbed their eyes, and "limbered up" sufficiently to get breakfast, after which they went to sleep again. It was good to see them sink into such profound slumber—a slumber which fell alike on man and beast. The mules were stretched on the grass, while the muleteers were leaning against the tent-poles in a state of absolute forgetfulness, sleeping like the Seven Sleepers. It was a camp of the dead. /

But in one tent there was wakefulness and watchfulness, and had been all night long, for there was great anxiety. One of our party was ill. Mrs. Adams, who is very slight of figure, and apparently incapable of much endurance, had borne all the fatigues of the march from Jerusalem, riding on horseback, facing the wind and the storm, and keeping up with any of us. But this ride over Mount Hermon was "the last straw"; and when we reached camp, she crept off her horse utterly exhausted. For a few hours we were in sore apprehension. Fortunately I recalled the name of a pupil of Dr. Post at Beirut, who is now the leading physician of Damascus, and a messenger was sent for him, and at three o'clock he came riding into camp. His judicious treatment, and the best of all medicine—a Sabbath day's rest—soon checked the alarming features of the case, and we were made unspeakably happy at the relief from a great anxiety./

With the feeling of relief there came a fuller enjoyment of the day of rest. Our messenger had brought back from Damascus letters which had been forwarded from Beirut, so that in our tents under the shadow of Mount Hermon, we were not far from home; at the same moment we were grateful for the recovery of a friend at our side, and for the safety of the dear ones far away. These mingled causes of gratitude glided into our hearts that still Sabbath afternoon. When we are thus grateful and happy, all things in nature seem to be in harmony with our spirits. The stream that ran before our tents sang to us of home—of our own dear New England, that land of mountain streams. On the other side of it was an enclosure filled with trees—at once an orchard and a garden— and it seemed as if we were smelling the apple blossoms; while the mighty dome above us, rising into the clouds, pointed upwards to the source of all good, from which all blessings descend, "as the dew of Hermon, and as the dew that descended upon the mountains of Zion, for there the Lord commanded the blessing, even life forevermore."/

# CHAPTER XVI.

## THE CITY OF DAMASCUS.

\ In approaching Damascus, one has in some degree the same feeling of wondering expectation, not unmingled with awe, as in approaching Jerusalem. It is (or claims to be) the oldest city in the world ; at any rate its history reaches far back into the twilight of antiquity. It is the real, if not the nominal, capital of Islam, from which marched the armies of Saladin, as still march the pilgrims to Mecca ; and it is said to be the most purely Oriental of cities. These things put us in a high state of expectation, as we mounted our horses to make our entry into Damascus. In one respect our mode of travel was changed : we had a road. We had left our rough mountain paths, and come down into the plain, and for the first time since we left Egypt had a highway over which a carriage could be driven. This was all-important for the one who most occupied our thoughts. A carriage had been sent out from Damascus by which our dear invalid was taken into the city with safety and comfort. Our riding party was farther reduced by the absence of Mr. and Mrs. Winter, who had left us on Sunday morning, he on horseback, and she in her palanquin. The rest of us were mounted as usual, and the broad road enabled us to ride abreast, instead of following one another in single file, as we had done in the bridle-paths over the hills. An extra horse in the company gave an opportunity for an extra rider. Among our servants was a fellow called Scander (short for Alexander), who by his good humor and merriment was the amusement of the whole party. He did not always have a chance to ride, but this morning, as there was an empty saddle, he wished to display his horsemanship, and boldly challenged Weeden, who was our champion rider, to a race, and even offered to wager a Turkish dollar on winning it, which he put into the hands of a clergyman of our party (I will not mention his name ; it was *not* Dr. Adams) to hold the stakes. So the coursers drew up, and we had John Gilpin's ride over again. Poor Scander, with his keffiyeh and his baggy trousers, looked like a bag of meal tossed on the horse's back, and as his legs spread far apart in the heat of the race, he "went flying all abroad." But Weeden, much better mounted, took the long strides, and easily came in ahead ; and then, with the dignity of a conqueror, magnanimously declined to receive the wager he had won. So ended the race, as all races ought to end, in leaving the parties as before. It was a harmless frolic, which left no bad blood behind it, but only both riders in a glow of ruddy health, and the rest of the party in a gale of laughter.\

After our fast riders had thus let off their spirits, we all jogged on quietly, observing the features of the country. The Plain of Damascus is like the Valley of the Nile, blossoming out of the desert, quickened by the same cause, a life-giving river. What the Nile is to Cairo, the Abana is to Damascus. Bursting from a pass in the mountains, it flows through the plain, converting into a garden what were otherwise a sterile waste. All this fertility has been

brought into being by the magic touch of the waters:
where they cannot reach, the desert remains. On our left
was a range of hills as barren as any we had seen in the
march to Sinai; while on our right was a country as rich
as the Delta of Egypt. As we approached the city, the
whole environs seemed to be embowered in shade. The
effect was the greater because of a sudden gathering of
clouds, which darkened not only the sky, but the earth
below, and gave a deeper and richer hue to this mass of
tropical vegetation. As we entered the outskirts of the
city, we rode through what seemed more like the green
country lanes of England than city streets. There are
miles of gardens, or rather of orchards, surrounding the
city on every side. The apricot and the pomegranate were
in blossom. Olives were in great abundance, interspersed
with walnuts; and groves of poplar, which is a favorite
wood. We think it a soft wood, but they find it hardy
(perhaps it is a different species), and as it grows rapidly,
it serves their purpose better than any other tree, and
whole forests of it are grown for timber.

I was disappointed in the situation of Damascus. I had
thought it lay in a deep valley; but it lies in a plain,
although at the foot of mountains, from which it has
the appearance of a broad valley. The traveller who
approaches it from the west will get his first sight of it
from the range of Anti-Lebanon, and as he looks down
upon it the view is much more imposing than if he
approached from the plain. A day or two after our
arrival, we rode out of the city, and ascended the hills on
the west to get this view. It was late in the afternoon,
and the sun was sinking behind the mountains, and threw
his last rays across the plain below, gilding the domes and
minarets of the great city. Here we could understand how
Mahomet, standing, according to the tradition, near this

very spot, should gaze and turn away, saying that God had promised to man but one Paradise, and he would not, by entering this on earth, endanger the loss of that in heaven.

But we are now riding into the city, under the shade of trees, by garden walls, and along the borders of streams, which at every step remind us of what has created all this Paradise : it is water bubbling up in fountains, and flowing in rivers, giving perpetual freshness to trees and grass and flowers, so that the city is literally set in a sea of verdure. /

Thus riding on through a succession of streets, we come to a gate which might be that of a fortress or a prison, so massive is it with wood and iron, nailed together with heavy spikes. In this grim portal is an opening a foot or two above the ground, and some four feet square, through which an outsider can gain admittance only by stooping. The gate was evidently contrived in view of possible dangers, when it might be necessary to barricade the entrance, and convert the interior into a fortress. We bent our heads, like captives passing under the yoke, and lifting our feet over the barrier below, found ourselves in the outer court of Dimitri's Hotel, the famous hostelry of Damascus. It was evidently a composite structure, made up of several different houses. To reach my room, I not only mounted a staircase, but passed along a corridor and *over a roof* into another house, which had been added to furnish more space for guests. It was the house of a Moslem : for the room was furnished with the lattices to the window always drawn around the hareem, through which the inmates can look without being seen. Thus put together piecemeal, the hotel is a rambling old barrack, but still pleasant enough inside, when one is in its open court, listening to the gentle plash of its fountain, and inhaling the fragrance of its orange trees.

But sweeter than orange blossoms or murmuring fountain, is the face of a friend.   I did not know a soul in
Damascus, and yet I had not been in that court five
minutes before I heard my name from the lips of a
stranger.   A stranger, and yet not a stranger : for he was
an American and a missionary—Rev. Mr. Crawford, who
gave me a warm grasp of the hand.   The sense of loneliness was gone.   From that moment, during our stay in
Damascus, he devoted himself to our comfort.   After
taking me to the postoffice and the telegraph office (which
are always the first calls to be made in a strange city), he
kindly offered to help us through the serious business of a
traveller, and under his lead Dr. Adams and myself set out
the same afternoon on a tour of exploration.   There is no
city in the world where one needs a guide more than in
Damascus : for its arrangement of streets is so intricate
and involved, with so many twists and turns, winding
about here and there in lanes and labyrinths, that a
stranger would be hopelessly lost.   Like most travellers,
we tried to "get our bearings," and form some idea of the
geography of the city by going first to " the street called
Straight," which we found to be very crooked ; yet it is not
difficult to reconcile its present appearance with its early
name.   At the beginning it was indeed a broad avenue a
mile long, running quite through the city, from the eastern
to the western gate, and lined with columns through its
whole extent.   But in time the habits of Eastern people
encroached on one side and the other ; it was crowded
upon by shops till the street thus invaded on both sides
was squeezed into a very small space ; and as the projections were by no means kept in a straight line, it has come
to be as full of nooks and angles and corners as any street
in the oldest quarter of London or Paris.

Of splendid architecture Damascus has none.   By those

who receive their impressions of Oriental cities from the
Tales of the Arabian Nights, it is sometimes confounded
with the capital of the magnificent Haroun al Raschid, and
looked upon as a city of "pleasures and palaces"—a gorgeous Oriental dream.   It *is* a dream, and only a dream—a
mirage of the desert, which fades away as we approach it.
In all Damascus I did not see a single specimen of fine
Saracenic architecture, of that airy lightness and grace
which one may see in the mosques of Cairo or Constantinople, in the Alhambra of Spain, or the mausoleums and
palaces of the Great Mogul in Agra and Delhi.    The
Great Mosque is indeed venerable for its antiquity, and
imposing from its vastness, as it rises above the wide
stretch of flat roofs, which we looked down upon from
the top of its tallest minaret ; and the Citadel shows its
front of battered walls, huge and grim ; but such structures do not make a city beautiful.   There are a few showy
houses of rich Jews, to which the stranger is taken, where
one finds always the same general construction—an interior court, paved with marble, surrounded by monotonous square rooms, lined with luxurious divans, on which
the master can recline in the heat of the day, and smoke
his narghileh, soothed by the murmur of the fountain in
the court.   But these are in fact, if not in name, mere
Summer-houses ; there is no provision for the rigor of
Winter, no open fire to blaze when the winds howl and the
snows fall on the heights of Lebanon, nor any of those
comforts which are to be found in the homes of England
and of America. /
   But if we do not find magnificence, we may at least find
that which is curious and quaint and old, and so we plunge
again into the wilderness of streets, winding and wandering
for hours, till we lose all the points of the compass, and are as
much at sea as if we had been in the middle of the Atlantic

Ocean. We are in a state in which we have conformed literally to the patriotic injunction given to Americans—to "know no North, no South, no East, no West." How then can I describe Damascus? How describe the indescribable? How give shape to that which shape hath none? How give a clear and intelligible outline of that which has been put together after no plan or architectural design; which has no centre from which its streets radiate, no squares or circles or crescents? But there is nothing like the conceit of a traveller. After the first day, when I had one or two points fixed in mind, I thought I could make my way alone; and coming back by Mr. Crawford's house, was about to take my leave to return to the hotel. He offered to send his son with me, but I declined, thinking it was not necessary, and that I could find my way through the streets. "Try it," he said with a smile; but he knew too well to let me try it, and insisted on sending a guide, who led me by the shortest cut, but yet by such winding streets that before we reached Dimitri's, I was as much lost as if I had been in an African forest. /

This bewilderment is apt to confuse a stranger, so that his first impression of Damascus is not one of enchantment. But after a day or two, he finds something fascinating in the musty old city, where even darkness and dirt are relieved by glimpses of color which light up the gloom of its decay. There is an endless picturesqueness in the costumes of the people, in their snowy turbans and flowing robes, beside which an American in his sober suit of black looks like an undertaker. The little narrow streets are full of life and activity. The sound of the artificers is heard under the long arcades. The workers in brass are here, whose curiously-wrought shields or trays remind me of those of Benares. Travellers of a military turn may gratify their tastes with Damascus blades or suits of old armor.

Those who have become so Oriental in their habits as to pass much of life in smoking, will find richly-jewelled pipes with amber mouthpieces ; while the ladies of a party are sure to be attracted by the many-colored silks. Altogether the bazaars of Damascus are as fascinating as those of Cairo or Constantinople, and over one and all might be written : " Whoso would shun temptation, let him not enter here ! " I thought I showed a Roman firmness in resisting the wiles of the adversary ; but when I was lured into the old khans, where Persian rugs are unrolled to the eye of the Western barbarian, my resolution gave way. Six years before I had bought nine rugs in Cairo, which I carried across the Atlantic as the spoils of Egypt ; and now to make it even, I had to take an equal number from Damascus. To be sure, I might have bought the same in New York ; but there was a certain satisfaction not only in having them *from* the East, but in buying them *in* the East, and in being able to trace them back to where they were made, in the far interior of Turkistan. Think of the pleasure of having under one's writing-table, as a rest for his feet, a rug that has been woven in Khorassan, and brought on the back of a camel across the desert from Bagdad! /

Of historical associations no Oriental city has more than Damascus. It boasts of being the oldest city in the world. Indeed, to make a " clean business " of the matter, it points to the red soil of this Plain as the very dust of the earth of which Adam was created! Leaving the Damascenes to amuse themselves with such fancies, we find the city spoken of in the Scriptures as early as the time of Abraham, " the steward of whose house was Eliezer of Damascus." Among the localities sacred alike to Jews, Moslems, and Christians, is the place where stood the house of Naaman, now fitly occupied by a hospital for lepers, since " he was a leper."/

To the Christian visitor Damascus has a special interest from its connection with the conversion of St. Paul. That his conversion took place at Damascus, is unquestioned; but that is not sufficient for devout believers : they must identify every locality with a mathematical precision. As we approached the city, we passed a church and convent which are said to mark the very spot where the Apostle was struck down by light from heaven, and heard a voice asking "Why persecutest thou me?" Within the city, Mr. Crawford took us to the house of Ananias, the scene of Paul's conversion. All that remains of the house is the cellar, in which is an altar, at which those who are overcome by the association can kneel and say their prayers. Outside of the walls the place is shown where the fugitive was let down in a basket. /

Damascus was for centuries a Christian city. The Great Mosque, like that of St. Sophia in Constantinople, was originally a Christian church. But time brought revolution. The scholar who studies the history of Christianity in the East, is sometimes tempted to ask whether it was for the corruption of the Eastern churches that a voice was at last heard in the holy place, as in the Temple before the destruction of Jerusalem, saying, Let us go hence? At last the spoiler came. But the importance of Damascus was in one way increased by the Mohammedan conquest, as it became the residence of the Caliphs; although it retained the Caliphate less than a century—from 673 to 762—when it was removed to Bagdad. But Damascus continued a great seat of Moslem power. Somewhat of the feeling of awe that one has at the tomb of Napoleon or of Frederick the Great, one has at the tomb of Saladin, the worthy antagonist of Cœur de Lion. Here in Damascus they keep his dust, in a mausoleum close by the Great Mosque, as England keeps the ashes of Wellington and of

Nelson under the dome of St. Paul's. No wonder that his tomb is a shrine for the faithful, as it was his mailed hand that finally struck down the Crusaders, and gave to Islam the undisputed mastery of the East for more than a thousand years. Now that his name has ceased to be the terror of Christendom, we can do justice to his memory. He was not only a great military chieftain, but a great ruler—at home in affairs of state as at the head of his army ; with a strong sense of justice, which restrained the fanaticism of his soldiers, and led him, when a conqueror, to treat his enemies with chivalrous magnanimity. /

In later centuries the importance of Damascus has diminished. After the conquest of Constantinople, the Caliphate was removed far from both Damascus and Bagdad, to the shores of the Bosphorus. But still Damascus remains one of the centres of Islam, where the Moslem spirit survives in its intensity. It is a furnace of Moslem fanaticism, of which it gave a terrible exhibition less than a quarter of a century ago. In the year 1860 its population were greatly excited by the murderous conflict in the Lebanon between the Druses and the Maronites—an excitement which rose to such a pitch that it broke out in one of the bloodiest massacres of modern times. For three days the city was given up to murder, and no less. than twenty-five hundred Christians, chiefly heads of families, were slain in cold blood! /

Mr. Crawford took us to see a venerable old man, who still bears the marks of sword cuts on his face, and who escaped almost by a miracle. Dr. Meshaka (father of the young physician whose skill we had tried) was a quarter of a century ago one of the most eminent of the Christians of Damascus, and hence was singled out as one of the first objects of attack ; but though wounded, he was not killed, but thrown into prison, apparently to be reserved, as a distinguished victim, for a more deliberate doom. From this terrible fate he was saved only by the intrepidity of Abdel Kader, who has for many years resided in Damascus. These two men, though one a Christian and the other a Moslem, had yet been attracted to each other by a certain nobleness in both, and had been fast friends; and when the rumor came—or it may have been only a suspicion, a fear or presentiment—that his friend was in peril, he flew to the rescue. Hastening to the authorities, he demanded to know where he was. They denied that he was in their power. But they were dealing with one whom they could not deceive. The old lion rose with a fury that could not be resisted. That imperious temper, which gave him such power over the tribes of the desert, cowed the assassins of Damascus, and they revealed the secret of the place of confinement, and conducted him to it, opened the doors, and Abdel Kader fell into the arms of his friend, whom he at once took under his own protection, and conducted to a place of safety. Seldom has history recorded a more touching instance of fidelity in friendship between men of different races and different religions. Nothing was ever told of Abdel Kader more to his honor. And now the venerable old man whom he saved from massacre, we saw in the midst of his family, in safety and in peace. We found him reading his Bible; he asked Mr. Crawford about the meaning of certain passages. He had passed the limit of four-score (he was eighty-four years of age), and was waiting, like an old saint, till his change should come. /

This massacre would have ended in the extermination of the Christian population of Damascus, had not the Turkish authorities, who were supposed to have encouraged the first outbreak, become alarmed, and found it necessary to put a stop to the shedding of blood; and after the slaughter had continued three days, they took families that had been decimated into the castle for protection. Here Mr. Crawford saw fifteen thousand poor creatures, in terror lest the gates should be thrown open and they be given into the hands of murderers, as had been done at Der-el-Kamar, where the Christian population was first disarmed by the Turks, and then left unprotected to the fury of the Druses, by whom twelve hundred were inhumanly massacred !/

This terrible outrage was not unavenged. It sent a thrill of horror throughout Europe, and French troops were speedily landed in Beirut. This stirred the Turkish authorities to do something, if they would not have the work of punishment taken out of their hands. One morning, as Mr. Crawford came into the streets of Damascus, he saw eight of the ringleaders hanging from the projecting beams of as many houses. Sixty-five were hanged that day, while a hundred and ten belonging to the army were shot, among whom was the Pasha of the city. By such prompt justice an end was put to these bloody scenes ; but the passion and fury were only checked, not destroyed : the fire is still smouldering in the ashes, ready to break out again with any fresh excitement. In the late war in Egypt there was a restless feeling among the population of Damascus, which was apparent to the eye of every foreigner. The Christians felt that they were again in danger—a danger that was averted only by the English victory at Tel-el-Kebir, and the entire collapse of the movement of Arabi Pasha. /

While thus kept in wholesome restraint by the terror of English arms, Islam is comparatively a harmless thing ; its chief manifestation of life being in the great pageant of the annual pilgrimage to Mecca. This is the event of the year in the Moslem calendar. A procession such as can be formed only in the East, of thousands mounted on

camels, files slowly through the city amid the enthusiasm
of its inhabitants, and streaming out of a gate which bears
the sacred name of the Gate of God, commences its long
journey towards Mecca.   Forty days does it keep on its
march, which, with the days spent in devotion at the tomb
of the prophet, and the forty days of return, make fully
three months consumed in this holy pilgrimage, which is
the great event of the pilgrims' lives. /

What is to be the future of Damascus?   Shall it have
no future save one of gradual decadence?   What is to
become of these old Oriental towns and decaying civilizations?   Of course Damascus will long continue to exist
on the face of the earth.   There will always be a city in
this Plain, whose natural fertility will support a large population; yet the city may decrease while others increase,
as its commerce drifts away from it to other points more
accessible to the trade of the world.   New lines of travel
by land and sea will cause other cities to spring up which
will cast into the shade a city that lives by the overland
trade of the desert.   Ships and steamers and railroad trains
will take the place of slow-moving caravans; and though
Damascus will still exist, it will not be the Damascus of old.

This gradual fading away of life seems to be typified in
the way in which the waters which create Damascus suddenly disappear.   They do not flow on to create other
cities, but sink into the earth.   It is a singular geographi-
cal fact that neither the Abana nor the Pharpar extends
beyond the Plain of Damascus.   About twenty miles from
the city, they lose themselves in a marshy lake which has
no outlet, but melts away in the sandy waste, so that at
that line verdure and vegetation disappear, while far in
the distance stretches the vast Syrian desert.   Is there not
in this something typical of these Oriental civilizations,
which have no force to flow beyond a narrow bound, or to

civilize any desert portion of the earth ; and of this ancient city which dates its existence, according to its credulous inhabitants, from the father of the human race? Damascus has had a great name in history : but its greatness is a thing of the past ; and in the coming centuries, though it may still live in the imagination of the world with the city of the Arabian Nights, its brightness will be only that of a splendid vision, glittering, yet fading, on the horizon of the East. /

/ Mahomet turned his back on Damascus before he entered it, but we *after* entering it and abiding in it three days ; and herein, with all respect for the prophet, I think we are the wiser, for though it is a quaint and picturesque old city, we do not find it so enchanting as to take away our desire for the heavenly Paradise, and are able to take our last look of it with a tranquil mind.  The horses are standing, saddled and bridled, at the gate, in front of which is a rabble collected to see the strangers depart, expecting perchance that the munificent Howadjis will rain backsheesh on the stones of the street.  One by one we put our heads through the sally-port of Dimitri's Hotel, and mount for the day, departing as we came, along the bank of one of the canals that bring the Abana into the city, and thus having the same pleasant sound of waters for our welcome and farewell.  Crossing a bridge, we turn westward over the great macadamized road to Beirut.  As soon as we touch it we come in contact with civilization.  In all Palestine there is not a carriage road, except the poor affair from Jaffa to Jerusalem ; but here is a highway as magnificent as any in Europe.  Of course such a road was

never built by the people of this country, nor by their
government. It is from beginning to end the work of
French engineers and French capital. The task was one
of great engineering difficulty, for the road had to cross
two ranges of mountains, Lebanon and Anti-Lebanon,
winding up and down their steep ascents and descents ;
but over all inequalities it was carried, and made as compact and firm to the very tops of the mountains as the
Simplon or any of the roads built by French or Swiss or
Italian engineers over the Alps. By this great highway
Beirut and the sea, which were four or five days distant
by caravan, are brought within thirteen hours of Damascus. This indeed was bringing Western civilization into
the heart of the East : it seemed as if we were in a city of
France, when we saw French diligences rumbling into the
ancient city of Damascus. Such a peaceful invasion of
the country ought not to alarm Arabs or Turks ; and yet
no doubt the road had a military purpose, as it was constructed after the massacres of 1860, which showed Europe
that it might become necessary for Christian powers to
interpose against any future outbreaks of Moslem fanaticism, when this would serve as a military road by which
troops could be conveyed swiftly to Damascus. It makes
European residents more comfortable to think that France
and England are thus brought so near to a city whose
streets not so long ago ran with Christian blood. /

Had we cared for speed, the diligence would have conveyed us in a night to the shores of the Mediterranean.
But preferring a more deliberate journey over the two Lebanons, we kept to our horses, and after an hour and a half
on the French road, turned to the right and began to climb
the hills. At first the road was very rough, but as soon as
we crossed the hills we struck into the valley of the Abana
(I prefer the good old Scripture name of this "river of

Damascus," to the modern name of Barada), and at once
came into a region of mingled wildness and beauty.  To
be sure there is but a narrow strip of verdure, only a few
rods in breadth, along the bank of the river ; but within
that space trees and plants of every kind grow with almost
tropical profusion.  The willows flourish by the water
courses ; and not willows only, but the fig tree and the
almond tree, the apricot and the pomegranate, and walnut
trees of great size, and whole forests of poplar, which are
grown for timber.

Riding along such shaded paths by the river side, we
came to the Fountain of the Abana, which, like the Jordan
at Banias, springs out of the heart of the earth ; and like
the Jordan, too, had its source honored from the earliest
times by a pagan temple, of which great blocks of stone
still remain.  The old arch which spanned it is broken,
but the river still rushes forth, as fresh and strong as when
nymphs and naiads sported in its waters.  We hope it
does not disturb the gods of fountains and of groves, that
this sacred stream is now made to turn a saw-mill ! /

In this green and shaded spot we spread our carpets
under the trees, and rested till the middle of the afternoon,
when we mounted and rode up the valley—a belt of living
green, made more beautiful by contrast with the rugged
mountains on either hand, which, by their height and
color, reminded me of the old red sandstone and red
granite of Sinai.  The whole appearance of the country
would have been as bleak and dreary as the desert itself,
were it not for this element of life, the water, which,
springing out of the rocks, and forcing its way through
the passes of the mountains, keeps up a perpetual warfare
with the mighty desolation.

We are now in the heart of the range of Anti-Lebanon.
Here and there villages are sprinkled among the hills,

whose sides are terraced, and along which the water is carried in channels for irrigation. Wherever it comes the mountain side blooms and blossoms at its touch. The path trodden by our horses was very narrow, but they picked their way among the stones with careful feet, and we had no slip or fall. It was not quite five o'clock when we came suddenly upon our camp. The pack mules had taken another road, and arrived before us. Our tents were pitched under a bank, where we were not only in the shadow of hoary mountains, but of hoary memories as well. On yonder hill which looks down upon us, is the tomb of Abel! How his body was recovered after the murder by Cain, and whether it was brought here by Adam and Eve, as chief mourners, we are not informed. Into these points it is better for the irreverent spirit not to inquire too curiously. /

But apart from this, there was enough in this quiet, peaceful spot to woo the traveller. We were camped on one side of a valley, on the other side of which was a little village, with the rushing Abana between—one of those mountain valleys which in a Catholic country, in Italy or Spain, would have been the seat of a convent or a monastery, from whose tower might sound the Angelus at sunset. How sweet would it have been at this hour to hear the vesper bell ringing among the hills! Here there is neither church nor convent, nor even a mosque with its minaret. Yet this place, so lonely, bleak, and wild, is not forgotten by God, nor is God forgotten by his children. The sun is just going down, and hark from the village below, from the top of one of the houses, I hear a voice which I never fail to recognize—it is the muezzin's call to prayer. To the devout Moslem the roof of a house is as good as the minaret of a mosque. It had a strange, weird effect, heard amid the silence of these mountains. And

who shall say that the offering was not as sincere as that
which ascends from Christian lands? Who am I to judge
the Moslem's prayer? Who can say that in these daily
prostrations there is not much of the true spirit of worship,
and that the prayers are not heard by Him who is the God
and Father of all mankind?

This little incident so touched me that it was with a
tender feeling that I turned away from that village of Suk,
on the site of the ancient Abila, the next morning, and
again began to climb the mountains. The roads were
rough, but through these mountain passes the Imperial
people hewed their way. We came upon the remains of
a Roman road and a Roman aqueduct. All day long we
followed up the Abana in its winding course, amid the olive
groves, while on the southern slopes plantations of mulber-
ries reminded us of a sunnier clime. /

As we had not a long march to-day, we stopped before
noon, tempted by the beauty of a spot of green turf under
a couple of grand old trees, beside a sweet, flowing spring
of water, where, spreading our rugs at the foot of the
trees, we took a siesta of nearly three hours. From this
resting place in the lap of the hills, we looked up and saw,
a thousand feet above us, peering out from under the trees,
the mountain village of Bludan, a favorite retreat from
Damascus during the heats of Summer, to which the English Consul and the English and American missionaries
resort. When we began our afternoon ride, for half an
hour we were scrambling over a very stony road, behind
the town of Zebedani, and at the entrance of one of the
loveliest plains of Syria—a plain which is cultivated with
that careful agriculture which one sees here and there
in the East, where men and women pick out every weed
from the fields as from a garden. There were extensive
orchards of apple trees in blossom. The hillsides were

covered with vineyards, in which I observed that it was a
custom of the people to lay their vines on the ground, perhaps to avoid the strong mountain winds, and also to get
from this close contact with the earth more moisture during the hot season, when there are no heavy rains to kill
the vines with damp and blight. /

At about three o'clock we crossed the water-shed of the
Anti-Lebanon range. We had reached the last of the
sources of the Abana, and henceforth the streams flow to
the west, in their course to the Mediterranean Sea. An
hour later we camped in another mountain valley, as fresh
and green as one could see in merry England in the month
of May. To be sure, we are here in the best season of
the year. When the Summer comes, much of this beautiful landscape will be dry and withered, burnt up with
the terrible heat ; while England, watered with continual
rains, keeps its freshness through the year. But for the
time one could hardly see more of beauty in any valley
of Wales or in the Highlands of Scotland. From the door
of my tent I look across the valley, perhaps a mile wide,
to a mountain which is cultivated nearly to the top. It is
not all green : for the variety of crops gives it a variety of
color. But there is a marked contrast in the two sides of
the valley. On our own, behind our tents, rise mountains
of rock, with scarcely a particle of verdure, save here and
there a stunted bush, while on a farther range lie large
patches of snow. Yet even here, scattered among the
rocks, are goats picking the scanty herbage. I see a flock
quite high up on the side of a mountain. At evening
they are driven down to the village beside which we are
camped, to be milked and to be sheltered for the night.
Here they come, followed by a troop of girls, all in white,
who have been watching them through the day, as Rachel
and Rebecca tended their flocks, and now bring them

home. Across the valley I hear the voices of children singing, and at sunset appears the prettiest of all rural pictures—children driving in the cows, which come from the valley, as the goats come from the mountain. At the moment perhaps every one of us recalled, as one at least repeated, the line of Kingsley :

" Mary, go and call the cattle home ! "

Such are bright pictures in all lands, whether in Syria or Scotland or Switzerland, in the valleys of the Lebanon or the Alps. /

Few things in our journey have given me more exquisite pleasure than these valleys of Anti-Lebanon. Beautiful in the rich verdure of the Spring-time, their beauty is enhanced by being set in a frame of mountains. As in the Swiss valleys, the intense green is heightened by contrast with the rocks and pines, and with the majestic and awful forms of nature : so do the mountains of Lebanon, on which the snow is still lying, look down on the loveliest of vales. Beauty goes hand in hand with plenty. It is a region of abundance, at least for the simple wants of the people. It is a relief to the eye to see. so much comfort and content here in the East, where we are so often pained by the sight of poverty and misery. /

And the people seem to be not only happy, but kindly. I know that the tribes of the Lebanon have a reputation for being fierce and warlike, as they showed themselves in the war that was waged in these mountains between the Druses and the Maronites. But now they had nothing to excite them, and to us they seemed to be a very simple folk. They are not only simple, but credulous and superstitious. When we arrived here, Mrs. Adams's horse was found to be ill. Floyd sent for a village doctor, who, although he prescribed for the poor creature, thought the beast bewitched by some one who had looked upon it with an evil eye, and burnt rags and broke crockery before it to exorcise the evil spirit! But we can forgive such follies to those who are kind at heart; and such they seemed to be, ready to respond to any act of civility. I never touch my hat to one—or rather my breast and forehead, according to the Oriental custom—without having the salutation returned. If I chance to be walking by the river side, and meet an old mountaineer, and put out my hand to him, his face lights up with a friendly glow, and we regret the want of language that prevents a freer expression of our mutual good will. /

One cannot but feel kindly towards such a people. The next morning the villagers were up at daylight milking the cows and the goats; and as we opened the doors of our tents, we were greeted with the same pretty sight as on the preceding evening—flocks and herds streaming in every direction to their pastures for the day, the cows to the meadows on the river's bank, and the goats to their perch among the rocks on the mountain side, both followed by troops of children, the gentle shepherds of this simple pastoral people. Blessings on them all! Long may they live among these mountains, untouched by famine : above all, in peace with their neighbors, so that these quiet vales may never again be wet with blood! /

With such impressions of the country and the people, we resumed our march. Before we left the valley, we passed orchards in which were the largest apple trees that I have ever seen, covered with blossoms, which filled the air with their perfume. For two or three hours we were riding through a gorge, where there was only a narrow path beside the rushing stream, which now flows westward, and empties into the sea near Sidon. At last we left the narrow pass, and struck directly up a very high hill, almost a mountain. Just before we reached the top, we met a couple of men heavily armed, one apparently the servant of the other. The superior was remarkably gracious and courteous in his greeting. Floyd said he was a famous bandit! But friend or foe, we had hardly time to return his salaam before there burst upon us a vision of beauty that might well make us forget the wickedness of man. It was the glory of Lebanon, which now came into full view on the other side of what we knew in an instant to be the Valley of Coele-Syria—one of the most beautiful valleys in the East, or in the world. /

When we left Damascus, our course had been directly to the West; but as we climbed the range of Anti-Lebanon, we turned gradually to the North, till now, as we descended the slopes, we were marching straight up the valley. The ride was long, as we tried to accomplish the distance to Baalbec in a single march. Had we divided the day, and made it in two rides instead of one, it would have been less wearisome. But we were in the saddle, without resting, for six hours. Some of the party, excited by the prospect of the great sight before us, pricked up their horses, while I lagged behind, keeping company with the palanquin of Mrs. Winter and the baggage train. At length we rose over a low hill, and saw in the distance the mighty ruins of Baalbec, and in another hour turned into the area of the wondrous pile, and passing through the long subterranean passage, dismounted in front of the Temple of the Sun, and sat down at the foot of columns whose enormous size recalled those of Karnak. /

And yet we were so fagged out by the day's ride, and by the whole week of fatigue in Damascus and on the mountains, that for an hour we were more occupied with our personal wants than with the splendid architecture around us. When the rugs were spread on the great porch, we crouched upon them in every posture of weariness, hiding behind the pillars to screen ourselves from the direct rays of the god to whom the Temple was dedicated. In front of us rose the six Corinthian columns of the other and still greater Temple, whose grace and beauty have delighted so many generations ; and yet even here our enthusiasm was held in check for the moment by hunger and weariness, which sometimes subdue the raptures of poetry. Pity that travellers have their share—some may think more than their share—of such infirmities! But at last hunger was satisfied, and fatigue began to abate. As soon as the tents were pitched in the grounds of the Temple, we threw ourselves on our couches, and took an hour or two of rest, after which all weariness was gone, and we awakened to the immensity and grandeur around us, and began to realize that we were in the presence of one of the wonders of the world. /

# CHAPTER XVIII.

## SABBATH MUSINGS IN THE RUINS OF BAALBEC.

/ If a traveller, when he first comes to Rome, instead of being driven to a modern hotel, could be permitted to pitch a tent in the Coliseum, he would find it easier to realize the grandeur of the Imperial city. He would not need to go to history; history would come to him: he would see it in the mighty walls reared eighteen hundred years ago, within which were crowded a hundred thousand spectators, and be a witness of the combats of lions and tigers, and of the fights of gladiators. Something of this vivid reality of the past we had as we camped within the ruins of the ancient Temple of Baalbec.

In those far-off times, when Syria was a province of the Roman Empire, in the second century of the Christian era, was reared in this beautiful valley of Coele-Syria, between the two Lebanons, a Temple which was designed to be at Baalbec what the Parthenon was in Athens, the glory and wonder of the Eastern world. Erected by the first of the Antonines, it was designed to be a monument of Roman greatness and power, that should endure to all generations. We have come to see how much of it remains after the lapse of seventeen centuries. /

I will not add another to the many descriptions of Baalbec. It is difficult to convey an idea, by mere architectural measurements, of structures so vast. Petty details rather detract from their full grandeur, which depends on their being taken in with the eye as a whole. A few general impressions must therefore take the place of minute description. When one rides into the great court, around which the temples are grouped, the first impression is of the vast scale on which the whole construction is planned. Everything is colossal. The area is larger than that of the Temple at Jerusalem. We may begin with the walls, which are half a mile around, and of such height as is rarely attained in the most tremendous fortress. When from within I climbed to the top, it made me giddy to look over the perilous edge to the depth below; and when from without the walls, I looked up at them, they rose high in air. Some of the stones seem as if they must have been reared in place, not by Titans, but by the gods. There are nine stones thirty feet long and ten feet thick, which is larger than the foundation-stones of the Temple at Jerusalem, dating from the time of Solomon, or any blocks in the Great Pyramid. But even these are pigmies compared with the three giants of the western wall—sixty-two, sixty-three and a half, and sixty-four feet long! These are said to be the largest stones ever used in any construction. They weigh hundreds of tons, and instead of being merely hewn out of a quarry which might have been on the site, and left to lie where they were before, they have been lifted nineteen feet from the ground, and there embedded in the wall! Never was there such Cyclopean architecture. How such enormous masses could be moved, is a problem with modern engineers. Sir Charles Wilson, whom I met in Jerusalem, is at this moment in Baalbec. Standing in the grounds of the Temple, he tells me that in the British Museum there is an ancient tablet which reveals the way in which such stones were moved. The mechanics were very simple. Rollers were put under them, and they were drawn up inclined planes by sheer human muscle — the united strength of great numbers of men. In the rude design on the tablet, the whole scene is pictured to the eye. There are the battalions of men, hundreds to a single roller, with the taskmasters standing over them, lash in hand, which was freely applied to make them pull together, and the king sitting on high to give the signal for this putting forth of human strength *en masse*, as if an army were moving to battle. A battle it was in the waste of human life which it caused. Who can estimate the fearful strain on all that host—how ranks on ranks fell down in the cruel task and died, only to be replaced by others, who were pushed on with the same remorseless tyranny! These Temples of Baalbec must have been a whole generation in building, and have consumed the population of a province and the wealth of an empire. Each course of stones must have been laid in blood and tears, as if it were a foundation of an altar of Moloch, who could only be appeased by a daily offering of human sacrifices. /

The interior is laid out like an Acropolis, on which several temples are grouped together, and all enclosed within the same wall. Of these the most perfectly preserved is the Temple of the Sun, the walls of which are still standing, although the heavy stone roof has fallen in. The style of architecture is that of a Greek temple, and shows where the Romans found their masters and their models. Laid out in the form of a parallelogram, and surrounded by columns, its general shape is that which has been so often copied from the Greeks, as in the Madeleine at Paris, and in Girard College in Philadelphia. It had a double row of columns in front, and a single row on either side and in the rear. Of these the greater part are fallen, except on the northern side, where the peristyle remains nearly perfect, thirteen out of the fifteen original columns being still erect. They are forty-six feet high, and support an entablature of large slabs of stone, which are richly sculptured in ornament, wreaths of foliage encircling the busts of emperors and gods. /

But the glory of Baalbec, upon which the pious Antonine lavished the wealth of Rome, is the Great Temple, of which there are far less remains than of the Temple of the Sun, but enough to show its magnitude and splendor. It was approached by a raised platform, or esplanade, 440 feet long by 370 wide, which led to the steps of the Temple. Of the vastness of the structure which rose on this Acropolis, some idea is given by the six Corinthian columns, sixty feet long and between seven and eight feet in diameter, which are still standing, and which from their position and height are conspicuous at a great distance across the plain, as one approaches Baalbec. What must have been the glory of that Temple when it stood complete, its roof of burnished gold reflecting the light of the rising or the setting sun, to the dwellers on the sides of Lebanon or Anti-Lebanon!

It was built to last for eternity. But alas for the dreams of ambition! It has been the spoil of ages. Attacked in the fury of the Moslem conquest, sacked by Tamerlane, and shaken by earthquakes, it has seemed as if man and nature had conspired for its destruction, till at last its columns lie prone upon the earth, or fallen one upon another, the whole a mighty ruin, a monument at once of the greatness and the littleness of man ; of the pride which seeks to perpetuate his power and his name ; and of the fate which overtakes the work of his hands. /

But other and graver reflections come to us here.  It is the day of rest : we are keeping our Sabbath amid these mighty ruins : and our thoughts take the form of a religious meditation.  These are not the ruins of Palaces, but of Temples, which show that there was in that day a belief in the higher powers.  The Antonine by whom they were reared bore the name of Antoninus Pius.  Though an Emperor on his throne, he was grave, serious, and devout, and devoted to the worship of the gods.  We are accustomed to think that those who reared these ancient temples knew how absurd was the worship for which they were intended, and built them only to embody certain ideals of their imagination, as the Greeks fixed in marble their conceptions of beauty in the statues and temples of Venus, or of Divine majesty and power in the temples of Jupiter.  But it is hard to believe that wise rulers would waste the resources of a kingdom to perpetuate a faith which they knew to be false.  They might indeed build temples, as the Pharaohs of Egypt built Pyramids, as their own monuments ; so that a Temple which bore the name of Jupiter should celebrate the glory of Cæsar, rather than the greatness of the god whom he professed to adore. (

\ But after all, who can say that Antoninus Pius, in building the Temple at Baalbec, did not *believe* in the gods as much as Leo X. believed in Christ when he drained the resources of Christendom to build St. Peter's at Rome ? Why should he not have so believed ?  Was there anything so ignoble in his belief as to be unworthy of the grave and thoughtful mind of the pious Emperor ?  One of these temples was devoted to the worship of the Sun, which, if any material object was to be adored, might well be worshipped as the Lord and Creator of life on the earth.  Was it not true then—is it not true to-day—that but for the great Luminary which daily rises in the East and

rejoices as a strong man to run a race, all life on earth
would cease to exist? Man himself would perish as quickly
and utterly as the meanest insect. Why then should he
not adore the Life-giver and Life-preserver?

Admitting this, another reflection follows. A Religion
which was mighty enough to build such temples, has perished from the earth. Who knows but that two thousand
years hence the Religion in which we believe may also
have passed away?

To this it may be answered that Christianity was
already in existence when these temples were builded,
and that while they are gone, it still lives. Then it was in
its weakness: now it is in its power. Then it was confined chiefly to the shores of the Mediterranean: now it
has gone into all the world. /

This is a plausible answer, but it is by no means
decisive, for other religions too have shown an extraordinary vitality. Brahminism and Buddhism are both older
than Christianity, and to this day they not only continue
to exist, but Buddhism probably holds in its dominion as
great a number of disciples as Christendom itself; while
Brahminism, if less in numbers, has a tenacity of life that
resists all the powers of Christian civilization. Skeptics
see the bearing of these comparisons. Not only men who
make a trade of their infidelity, in sporting their wit in
popular lectures, but thoughtful students of history, confess to the force of this argument, which produces on them
the same effect that the revelations of science do upon the
minds of scientific men. It will not do to make light of
this cause of unbelief. Reading, studying, and reflecting,
many scientific men of Europe and America fully believe
that the progress of science in the course of one or two
centuries will dispel the last lingering faith in the Divine
origin of our religion. In their philosophic eyes, our

Christian faith is but one form of human credulity, which must run its course and then disappear. Timid Christians may lament it, but the result is said to be as inevitable as the course of the sun in the heavens./

To these sombre forebodings it will not do to reply with looks of horror, as if historians and men of science were atheists and blasphemers. It is better to admit frankly that Christianity *will* share the fate of the ancient mythologies, unless it has in itself the evidence of its truth. Those who are so zealous to defend it, must not be afraid of discussion or argument, but welcome light from every source. Instead of fearing science, they ought to hail it as the best friend of religion. Everything which throws light on the laws of nature, reveals the power and wisdom of God. While we are not to be disturbed by mere flippant attacks, by caricature or ridicule, yet if anything which we have been accustomed to accept be fairly disproved, we are simply to readjust our faith to the new evidence. No man of intelligence who has mastered even the rudiments of geology, can doubt the great antiquity of our globe. The proof lies all round us in the everlasting hills. When we come to see this, and reëxamine the sacred record, we find that the difficulty was not in the Bible, but in our own ignorance, in our narrow and petty interpretation. As we see more clearly, all things come into harmony. Earnest seekers after truth, we cry with the dying Goethe "Light! light! more light!" We may not build a Temple to the Sun, but we shall welcome light from every source, whether from the orb of day, or from him who is the Source of all light, and who has given his creatures intelligence to discern the truth, even as he has made great lights in the firmament—the sun to rule the day and the moon to rule the night. /

Further still, if Christianity is to live, it must prove its right to live by deeds of goodness and charity, which shall show it to have come from God. It must attest its Divine origin by the life which abides in it, and which it imparts to its disciples. I confess that I have seen in the East much which calls itself Christian, which in faith differs little from the ancient mythology, and which in the life it produces, is no better than the ancient paganism. If I had to choose between the piety of Marcus Aurelius, or Antoninus Pius, and many of the types of Christianity which I see here, I should not hesitate a moment. In Jerusalem itself the contrast is not to our advantage. In the Church of the Holy Sepulchre, where Greeks and Latins meet together to celebrate the death and resurrection of their common Lord, they meet not in mutual love, but glaring at each other in hatred, which they do not attempt to conceal, and Moslem soldiers stand guard over them, to prevent angry strife in the very temple of God! Not so is the world to be won to him who is the Master of us all, but by a Religion founded in truth, supported by every argument of science and philosophy, and above all, illustrated in lives of purity and peace and love, which shall cause the moral wildernesses to bud and blossom as the rose. /

Such were the musings of that Sabbath day in the ruins of Baalbec. After such grave meditations, it was a relief, as the day was drawing to a close, to leave the ruins, and take a walk through the village : for there is a village here of two or three thousand inhabitants—a village not poorer than other Syrian villages, and which would appear quite respectable were it not thrown into insignificance by the contrast with the remains of the masters of the world. But if the people are poor, they can be happy, as we saw by a very pretty scene. Following a small stream which flowed with a rapid current, we came to a bit of green sward sur-

rounded by the waters like an island.   Here Floyd had
proposed to pitch our camp, but we preferred the grounds
of the Temple.   Yet no one could find fault with such a
camping-ground.   It is a resort of the people of the village, who were here in numbers, well dressed, and enjoy-
ing the quiet evening and the open air with their children.
As we came back to our camp, we stopped at the Maronite
church in the village, which is very small, and has but few
worshippers.   It is a feeble and glimmering light in the
midst of so much darkness.   A better hope we have from
the Protestant schools introduced as an offshoot of the
American Mission in the Lebanon, which are well attended,
and give hope that Baalbec, if never again the seat of Imperial grandeur, but left only to be the site of a Syrian
village, may yet be the abode of intelligence, of content-
ment, and of peace. |

The day was ended, but the night drew on, which was
even more fitted to put one into a mood of sober musing
than the day.   As the sun was setting, I went up on the
wall, and sat a long time watching the light in the west as
it faded over mountain and plain.   Hardly had the sun
gone down when the full moon rose in the opposite quarter of the heavens, shining through the rents in the gray
old walls with a soft light that gave them a strange, un-
earthly beauty ; while the columns that were still standing
cast long shadows on the solitary place — shadows that
seemed to the quickened fancy like the ghosts of old
Romans come to revisit the scene of their ancient splendor.   But they are only ghosts.   The Romans are gone ;
the legions are departed ; we hear their tramp growing
fainter and fainter in the distance, and at last dying away
like the hollow wind.   What a monument of human vanity
is this desolation !   How it rebukes the pride and ambition, not only of kings and conquerors, but of nations. /

As for individuals, we shall disappear, as those shadows disappear with the rising sun. These walls which have stood for centuries will remain for centuries to come ; but we shall pass away and be no more seen. But there is that which shall abide when man and all his works have perished. The city of God which is above is built of spiritual stones, which will not crumble with the ages. In the Great Mosque of Damascus is an old Greek inscription, placed there in Christian times, and not removed by its Moslem masters, but still embedded in its walls, which we may perhaps interpret as a prophecy of coming events in the East, as well as of that realm which is universal and eternal : " Thy kingdom, O Christ, is an everlasting kingdom, and thy dominion endureth to all generations."/

# CHAPTER XIX.

THE VALLEY OF COELE-SYRIA—CROSSING MOUNT
LEBANON.

If one were to choose a day in all the round year,
which should be the brightest and best, on which to begin
a journey or to end it, would it not be the first of May?
So we thought as we struck our tents the next morning,
and mounted our horses. But bright expectations are not
always realized. At our setting out a rainbow in the west
gave ominous conjecture of what the day might bring
forth, and hardly had we left the ruins of Baalbec before
the darkening sky warned us that our apprehensions were
to be realized. But nothing could hide the beauty of the
landscape. On this first of May we were to enter the
Garden of Eden, to the description of which few valleys
answer more than this of Coele-Syria. It is probably the
bed of an ancient lake, which has left a bottom as smooth
and level as when the waters flowed over it. Not only
is it of great natural fertility, but richly cultivated. It is
dotted with villages, which are no longer confined to the
hills. Fields of wheat and barley remind an American of
the abundance of our Western prairies. As the soil contains a great deal of iron, it turns up red, while the spring-

ing wheat gives to the fields the richest green. This
contrast of color is one of the beauties of the valley. On
our right is the range of Lebanon, whose foot-hills advance
into the plain, keeping the waving line of beauty in their
rounded slopes; while behind and above them, as well as
on the opposite side of the Plain, is the background of the
mountains. /

The effect of all this was greatly enhanced by the
threatened storm. Though the clouds did not burst, yet
great masses darkened the sky, and as they swept across
it, cast their shadows on the sides of the mountains. At
first fell a few scattering drops, and then came full in our
faces gusts of wind with heavy rain, against which we had
but a feeble protection. We put up our umbrellas, which
was like hoisting flags at half-mast, and rode on. Four
hours of this made us quite willing to rest, when we
reached the village of Muallaka, and found shelter in a
house which had little furniture except matting on the
floor, travellers being expected to provide not only food,
but bedding, if they rest for the night, as in the dak-bun-
galows of India. However, if the rooms were bare, they
were dry, and gave us a feeling of comfort. This village,
though little known to the world, has one possession which
of itself were enough to confer distinction upon it, the
sepulchre of Grandfather Noah; and to make the most of
it, they have stretched him out to his full proportions, his
tomb being two hundred feet long! Even with this, the
patriarch is somewhat cramped: for it is said that his
knees are bent, and his lower limbs planted straight in the
ground! These fables are devoutly believed by the Moslems, with whom the tomb is an object of great veneration. /

By the middle of the afternoon, we reached Stoura, the
midway station on the French road from Damascus to
Beirut; and as soon as our horses' hoofs struck that, we

had a firm path under our feet, and a line of telegraph over
our head—the double sign of civilization.   That long line
of telegraph poles which has marched up the other side of
Lebanon, and now goes striding over the valley of Coele-
Syria, to climb Anti-Lebanon, and descend into the Plain
of Damascus ; does not stop there, but stalks away across
the Syrian desert to Bagdad and to Persia, and thus con-
nects Europe with Central Asia.

But the great sign of civilization is the road itself, with
the traffic which passes over it in huge covered vans, like
those known in America as Pennsylvania waggons, each
one of which is drawn by three mules, and will carry the
loads of half a dozen camels.   They generally go in companies of a dozen or twenty, which together would transport as much as a large caravan ; and as they are always
in sight, going up and down the mountains, they present
the appearance of the transportation train of an army. |

We did not stop for the night at Stoura, but pushed on
a mile or two up the side of Lebanon, and camped on a
green spot, from which we had the whole Plain of Coele-
Syria at our feet.   Our tents were pitched none too soon.
Hardly were we under shelter, when the rain, which had
been fitful all day, came down heavily.   Night set in dark
and gloomy.   But what soldier ever cared for the elements
the last night of a campaign?   Nothing could check the
flow of our spirits so near the end of our journey.   Our
long march was nearly over.   This was our last night in
tents, and we were in a merry mood as we gathered round
our table, even though the rain was pouring in torrents ;
nor did it disturb our rest, though it kept on pouring all
night long.   A little before morning the clouds broke
away, and the sun came out gloriously ; and when we
broke camp, our tent life was over. |

We were early in the saddle for our last ride, and

started briskly up the mountain. What a pleasure to ride with free rein on such a road as this, instead of picking our way over stones among the rough bridle-paths of Palestine! But we are not alone on the march. The movement of baggage waggons, which has not ceased during the night, keeps up its steady rumble. The waggons that have to climb the mountain strain hard and move slowly, while those descending come down rapidly. There is something very impressive in this endless march and countermarch, this moving to and fro of busy life, keeping its endless course along the highways of civilization. In this traffic are the products of all nations and all countries, from the farthest East to the farthest West. Nor is America unrepresented. The most conspicuous object in these baggage waggons, is American petroleum. On the top of all the European wares stares at me the sign of "Pratt's Astral Oil : warranted not to explode"! The oil drawn from the wells of Pennsylvania finds its way to the cafés and bazaars of Damascus and Bagdad, and even to the tents of the Bedaween ; so that whatever be said of the moral influences which America sends to these shores, in one very practical and material way she furnishes the illuminating element to light up the darkness of the East.

The diligences from Damascus and Beirut pass each other—that which is climbing having extra mules harnessed to it, to drag it up the steep ascent ; while that which has crossed the summit comes down the mountain at full speed, swinging round the windings of the road in a way that reminded me very vividly of a passage of the Alps years ago, before the tunnel was bored under the Mont Cenis, when, with similar speed, we came rushing down into the valleys of Savoy.

In a couple of hours we had reached the top of the mountain, and turned our horses to take a last look at the

valley of Coele-Syria, which was spread out before us.
There are few fairer spots on the earth's surface.  Here,
and not at Damascus, is the Paradise from which Mahomet
might well have turned away.  Though the valley be not
so broad as the Plain of Damascus—it is only three or four
miles wide—it is more beautiful, as the mountains come
nearer.  Lebanon and Hermon beckon to each other
across the plain.  Seldom does the eye rest on a more
glorious object than that snow-crowned head of Hermon,
as it stands clear and white in the morning sky.  With a
lingering look, we turned away from a vision which we
shall never look upon again, but which we can never
forget. \

And now we begin to descend the western slope of
Lebanon.  The way is long, for the road winds in and out,
to make an easy and gradual descent.  As we turn hither
and thither, there opens before us a wide prospect of forest
and mountain, while every moment comes nearer and
clearer the view of a great city, and of the sea beyond.
I had seen the Mediterranean but twice before, at Gaza and
from the top of Carmel, since I landed at Alexandria. \

We stopped but once for rest on the mountain side,
riding into the yard of a khan, from which—the yard—
(and it was not a court-yard or door-yard, but a barn-yard)
there was a grand outlook toward the sea.  As we stood
admiring the view, a horseman came up the road, who had
the dress of a European, and we supposed to be a gentleman from Beirut taking an airing on the mountains, when
he rode into the yard and called my name.  It was Mr.
Dale of the American Mission, who was on his way from
Beirut back to his home in Zahleh, a large village in the
Lebanon.  We detained him for luncheon, and sat down
together, squatting on our mats in the Eastern fashion.
He made but a brief halt, as he had far to ride ; but in

that short time his earnest missionary spirit left a pleasant impression upon us all. A native of Philadelphia, with the education of a scholar, and a refinement of manners that would seem to make much in Oriental habits repulsive to him, he has chosen the life of a missionary, not from a hard sense of duty, but because it is the work which he loves, and enters into with enthusiasm. " When," I said to him, "are you going to return to America? Do you not pine for a sight of Philadelphia?" "Philadelphia!" he answered. "What is Philadelphia compared to Zahleh?" That is the stuff that American missionaries are made of, and such are the men who have made bright so many spots on the sides of Lebanon. \

The ride was easy now that we were coming down the mountain. The horses stepped quickly, and with each descending curve of the road the outline of the coast became clearer, till we could see the long stretch of sandy beach and the white caps of the waves breaking on the shore. There, on a promontory jutting into the sea was Beirut, the roofs of its houses glistening in the sun. The approach is through a succession of olive groves, which cover the plain and reach far up the mountain side, making the wealth of the villages which are perched upon the rocks ; and through plantations of mulberry-trees, which show that silk culture is one of the great industries of the country. Near the city are groves of pine trees, which are not common in Syria, but which are planted here to furnish a cool retreat in the heats of Summer. So we rode on till we were within about two miles of the city, when I saw coming a face that looked familiar, and soon recognized a voice that I had often heard among the rocks of Sinai. It was Dr. Post, who had come out to meet me. I had been " stopped on the road" once before in his company, but that was by robbers on the desert. Then he told me not to get off from my camel ; but now he bade me dismount. I was sorry to say good-bye to the faithful beast that had brought me from Jerusalem, but I confess that after weeks and months of rocking and jolting on horseback and camel-back, I was not sorry to descend from this elevation, and to "come up into the chariot." Remembering my anxiety at Gaza for news from my family, he had brought with him letters and a telegram from Venice, to cheer me with good tidings on my second return to civilization. (

And then he took me to his home. Having some little means of his own, he has chosen to use them in the wisest way that a man can, in providing for his family a house after his own taste. It is a modest English cottage, with only the addition of the broad veranda, which is as indispensable in an Eastern house as in an Indian bunga-low ; while the interior, in its comfort and convenience, is quite American. The love of flowers betrays itself in the perfume that greets us as we drive in at the gate. Vines overrun the walls and encircle the doors and win-dows, and fill the air with fragrance. But the glory of the house is its position, on a bluff, from which one can look off, like Elijah's servant from the top of Carmel, "over the wide expanse of the Mediterranean Sea." My windows take in the whole horizon of waters, with snow-capped mountains in the north. One can hardly realize, except in coming out of the wilderness, the exquisite charm of such a dwelling. What is the excitement of tent life compared with this sweet domestic repose ? With all the poetry of the mountains or the desert, I prefer civilization ; and am content to dwell no more in "tabernacles," like Abraham, Isaac, and Jacob, when I can exchange them for the order and taste, the comfort and the refinement, of an American home.\

# CHAPTER XX.

## BEIRUT—AMERICA IN THE EAST.

/ The traveller who makes Beirut the terminus of his journey through the Holy Land, will be apt to feel that he has kept the best until the last. It is in some respects the most attractive city in the East. Its position unites almost every element of beauty. As Byron pictures the scene of one of the great battles of history in the lines

> The mountains look on Marathon,
> And Marathon looks on the sea ;

so we may say of the modern commercial capital of Syria. Its site has been chosen on account of its secure harbor for ships, while behind it and around it sweeps the chain of Lebanon. It is a constant pleasure to turn the eye to that glorious background of mountains. It is not as in India, where one has to travel hundreds of miles over the hot and sultry plains, to reach the Hills. They are in full sight, but two or three hours distant. The residents of Beirut, in Summer, take up their quarters in the villages that hang on the side of the mountains, embowered in olive trees. Here the missionaries have their retreats. Dr. Post and Dr. Dennis have adjoining cottages, eyries from which they can look down on their city homes. \

But the great beauty of Beirut is the sea. It stands on a point of land which projects so boldly that the sea is on three sides of it, and almost girdles the city with a zone of silver. There it is morning, noon, and night—at sunrise and sunset, in twilight and moonlight and starlight, in calm and storm, enchaining the eye, now by its beauty, and now by its majesty and power. \

The sea brings commerce, and Beirut being at the head of the Mediterranean, has a large trade with all the countries along its shores, sending its olives and silks to Italy and France, to England and to America. Her merchants are princes, whose wealth appears in the stately mansions, which rise on the hillsides that enclose the city.

Being thus connected by commerce with Europe, Beirut is half a European city. Here for the first time in Syria, one finds paved streets, through which he can drive in a carriage, and good roads out of the city, with many other signs of European order and civilization.

It is one of the few parts of the Turkish Empire that is decently governed. This is the fruit of European intervention. After the massacres of 1860, France and England insisted that the Christian population should not be left to the fanaticism of the Druses and other Moslems, and assumed a sort of protectorate over the Lebanon, in consequence of which it has at this moment an excellent Governor in the person of Rustem Pacha, of whom the missionaries speak in the highest terms.* \

---

* I regret to be obliged to add, that within the past year, when his term of office expired, owing to the opposition of France, Rustem Pacha was not reappointed Governor of the Lebanon. The new appointment was the subject of intrigues at Constantinople, and it seems almost a miracle that, as the issue of this conflict of parties, the Porte has sent one who has the reputation of being a man of integrity, justice, and courage. \

The commercial importance of Beirut brings here not only the Consuls of different countries, but a large number of foreign residents, bankers and merchants, who form a very agreeable community. With this European life is introduced another element not less important to the future of the East—Christian institutions. The Catholics are here in force with their large convents and seminaries; but their presence need not alarm us; we need not fear any rivalship in well-doing. Let them do all the good they can. However active and self-denying their Sisters of Charity may be, they cannot surpass in devotion the Deaconesses of Kaiserswerth, who are here in the hospitals, giving themselves to the care of the sick and the poor. Such angels of mercy bless the world wherever their footsteps come. |

Of course, the hand of England is here, as it is everywhere : her institutions are scattered over the globe. The last morning that we were in Beirut there was a gathering of the children of the famous schools of Mrs. Mott. As a number of strangers, English and American, stood on the steps of the large mansion, which from its position on the hill-side overlooks the city and the bay, and saw a thousand children marching through the spacious grounds singing their songs and waving their banners, all felt that they might have been witnessing a Sunday-school celebration in England or America. It was one of those happy scenes which give us hope that the next generation will be better than their fathers.

While recognizing the noble efforts of different countries, it is natural that an American should feel a special interest in those which originated in his own country, to which I refer as showing that America, though so far away, has a legitimate influence in the East. Although not one of the Great Powers which assume to regulate the

affairs of Europe and of the Eastern shores of the Mediterranean, she has a position of her own, which carries with it
very great influence.   True, she has no "Eastern policy,"
except the policy which she has towards all nations—that
of peace and good will.   She did not join with England
and France in fighting the battles of Turkey in the Crimean
War, in which they rendered a doubtful service to civilization.   In a preceding war of Turkey the sympathies of
America were wholly against that power, and on the side
of Greece ; but she took no part in the struggle beyond
that of receiving and protecting refugees flying from the
massacre of Scio.   She has entered into no Eastern war :
she has sent no army to these shores, and no fleet into
these waters.   Once indeed the United States intervened
in the Mediterranean ; but not for any selfish, or merely
national, interest, but in the interest of the whole world,
against the Barbary pirates, who for three centuries had
levied tribute on the commerce of all nations—a tribute to
which America was the first to oppose a determined and
successful resistance.   In 1815 Commodore Decatur won a
brilliant victory, which brought the haughty Dey of Algiers
to terms, and compelled him to recognize the flag of the
United States as inviolable—a work which was followed up
the next year by the English fleet under Lord Exmouth,
which bombarded Algiers, and compelled the Dey to
release all Christian slaves.   Some years afterwards American ships rendered a like service in pursuing the pirates
who hid themselves among the islands of the Greek archi-
pelago.   But this hunting of outlaws on land or sea is
not war against a country or a government, so that it is
literally true that, from the foundation of our Republic, its
relations with the Eastern world have been those of peace
and friendship. /

With such a policy of non-interference with other

nations—a policy declared from the beginning and followed up in all her history, how is it that America has obtained a position or acquired influence in the East, where influence generally goes with the display of military or naval 'power? Perhaps her influence has been partly owing to the fact that she has *not* made any such display of force. Having no political designs, she has not been an object of suspicion. But it has not been this alone. More powerful than the action, or non-action, of the government, has been the silent influence of individual men.

More than half a century ago, while the war with Greece was still raging, American missionaries were sent to Constantinople, Smyrna, and Beirut, and into the interior of the Turkish empire. They came, not as emissaries of their Government, but as Christian teachers. They planted schools; they gathered churches; they were the friends of the poor, whom they often fed in the time of famine, and to whom they ministered in sickness, facing the horrors of the cholera and the plague that they might give them relief. Thus in the course of a generation they made their way into the hearts of the people, and won universal confidence and respect. /

Of these messengers of peace, some went up to the top of Lebanon, where their feet were beautiful upon the mountains. There was one who was fitly called the Cedar of Lebanon — he was of such commanding presence that he might well be likened to one of the goodly cedars. This man, Simeon H. Calhoun, who might have held a position of honor in his own country, spent more than thirty years on Mount Lebanon, teaching Arab boys, that when they were grown to be men, they might become pastors and teachers. Years passed before he could see the fruit of his labor; but after a generation he was able to say that "From his academy on Mount

Lebanon had gone out teachers carefully grounded in natural philosophy, the lesser mathematics, geography, history, Arabic, and especially the Bible. These teachers were in Jaffa, Gaza, in the land of Moab, in Ramoth-Gilead, in Damascus. The teacher of the high school in the latter city was one of his pupils. They were carrying the Christian Scriptures and the elements of education among their people all over the Holy Land."

The influence of such a man could not be confined to a school, a village, or a community. The people of the East are impressed by anything that betokens peculiar sanctity, and they were awed by his grave and reverend aspect, and still more, by his life. There was in him something so unworldly, that they revered him as a saint. Such was the influence he acquired over them, and such their confidence in him, that when civil war broke out in the Lebanon between the Maronites and the Druses, and raged with terrible ferocity—when the nights were lighted up with the burning of villages, and massacre on one side provoked massacre on the other—both sides came to him for protection, and brought their precious things, and stored them under his roof, feeling that they were safe under his care. Was there ever a greater tribute to the power of character over infuriated men ?/

It was the desire of this noble man to die on Mount Lebanon, and to sleep among the people whom he so much loved. On his last visit to America a friend urged him to remain in his own country, where his long experience in missions might benefit the Church more than his services abroad; but he answered "No; there are two cedars on Lebanon just far enough apart for my body to lie between them, and there will be my resting-place." But this was not to be. He had come back to America to die, and his body rests in the soil of his native land. But he has left on Mount Lebanon, and in all the East, the memory of his goodness, and the rich inheritance of his beloved name.

I speak of this missionary rather than others because I knew him best. When I was in College he was my teacher, and he has always been in my memory as the very type of Christian manliness. But there were others of like spirit associated with him. The Mission cemetery in Beirut holds their dust. There sleeps Eli Smith, who accompanied Dr. Robinson in his exploration of the Peninsula of Sinai and of the Holy Land. Such were the men who founded the Syrian Mission, which they left as the fruit of their labors, a legacy to those who should come after them. /

With such a history of fifty years behind it, it is not surprising that this Mission is so thoroughly organized, with every aid to a work that is designed to be extensive and permanent. Dr. Eddy, one of the old veterans of the Mission, has charge of the Press, and edits a paper in Arabic, besides preaching in a chapel in another part of the city. Dr. Jessup is the pastor of the native church, and by his eloquence, which is equally marked whether he speaks in English or in Arabic, draws crowds to hear him. Near his house is a seminary for Arab girls under the charge of Miss Everett, assisted by Miss Jackson, and by Miss Thomson, a daughter of the author of "The Land and the Book."/

But the chief glory of this Mission, and the brightest spot in Beirut, is the Syrian Protestant College, founded by American liberality. Its corner-stone was laid twenty years ago by William E. Dodge of New York. Never was an institution more wisely planned, or more successfully conducted. Though but twenty years old, it will take rank with any American college that has not had a longer existence, and indeed with many that are much older. The President, Dr. Bliss, has nursed it from the day of small things with admirable tact and judgment. In the starting of it, and in all the early years of its history, he acknowledges himself greatly indebted to the daily counsel and efficient aid of Rev. David Stuart Dodge, whom not only Dr. Bliss, but all the missionaries here regard as a man whose extreme modesty hides from all but those who know him intimately his great ability. Thanks to their combined efforts, the College was a success from the beginning. The President has gathered about him a staff of professors and teachers such as would make the reputation of any college. /

Indeed there is one man who in his own department has no superior and no equal. Dr. Van Dyck is, by the confession of European scholars, the first Arabic scholar living. He is the chief translator of the Bible into Arabic —a work begun by Dr. Eli Smith, who wrought upon it until his death, when the burden fell on Dr. Van Dyck, who gave to it twelve years, and carried it through to the end. The translation is said to be one of the best in any language. For the benefit of students, he has published a valuable work on Arabic Prosody. But he is not a mere Arabic scholar. In other departments the extent and variety of his attainments is quite extraordinary. He is a physician, a chemist, a mathematician, and an astronomer. He has published a book on Chemistry (of course in Arabic), and several on Medicine, one of which, on Pathology, is a work of a thousand pages. There is one on Physical Diagnosis, and he has another ready for the press on Diseases of the Eye. His book on Geography has gone through four editions. He has published an edition of Euclid, and a work on Algebra (two editions); and a large work on Mathematics, including Logarithms, Plane and Spherical Trigonometry, Mensuration, Surveying, and Navigation; and also a work on Astronomy, and has now ready for the press a second book on Practical Astronomy, and still another on the Geography of the Heavens. There is a small Observatory connected with the College, where he amuses himself, when wearied with his other labors, in watching the stars. Such an example of intellectual activity, in so many departments, is very rare in any country. While attending to all these departments of the College, he takes his full share in the work of the Hospital, alternating with Dr. Post. Meeting him one day as he returned from this duty, he said with a smile: "I have had only seventy-five cases to-day; sometimes I have a a hundred and twenty-five."/

So perfect a master of the language is Dr. Van Dyck that when dressed in the costume of the country, as he is sometimes on a journey, he might be mistaken for a native, as indeed he was on one memorable occasion, when it nearly cost him his life. In the war of 1860, when the Druses and Maronites were fighting in the Lebanon, he was sent for as a physician to care for the wounded; and prompt at every call of duty, started at once, not even waiting for an escort or a guard, thinking himself sufficiently well known to be able to pass anywhere. But he fell into the hands of a party who did not know him, and who could hardly believe that a man who was such an Arab in his speech, was not a native of the country; and if so, and not on their side, he must be an enemy, and it might have gone hard with him had not one who did know him suddenly appeared and rescued him out of their hands. This incident had a sequel worth repeating. In the crowd of those who were ready to put him to death, was one man whom he thought he recognized, but who, instead of befriending him in his extremity, seemed to be urging the others on. Several years after, who should come into the hospital at Beirut to be treated for some affection of his eyes, but this very fellow! The Doctor knew him at once as the man whom he had met in

quite other circumstances, and calling him by name, said
"Ah ha! are you here?" at which the wretch began to
tremble and beg for mercy. But the good Doctor soon
relieved his fears. "Don't be afraid," he said ; "I shall
not do you any harm"; and bending over him with as
much tenderness as if at the couch of a friend in similar
need, he ministered to his relief, trying to save from blindness the man who had wished to shed his blood. Was ever
an act more in the spirit of the Divine Master?

Associated with this grand old man are half a dozen
younger men, who are fast making proof of their ability,
and giving promise of distinction. /

Connected with the College at an early day was a Medical Department, of which Dr. Post, my companion on the
Desert, has been from the beginning the inspiring soul,
and which has had a very remarkable success. Of Dr.
Post I can hardly speak without seeming to be influenced
by personal feeling. It is true he is my friend, and very
dear to me, and I could not, if I would, take his measure
"critically." But I do not think I am unduly influenced
by friendship, when I regard him as one of the most useful men in the East. Certainly he is one of the most inde-
fatigable men I have ever known. Slight in figure, he is a
bundle of nerve and muscle, quick in motion, of great
physical activity and endurance, a splendid horseman,
riding like an Arab, if need be, to meet some call of duty ;
doing everything rapidly and at the same time well. Being
in his house nearly a week, I sometimes thought it would
be the best reply to those who think missionaries have an
easy time of it, if I could keep a chronicle of the number
and variety of the duties to which he attends in a single
day. He is the first surgeon in Syria. If he were to give
himself up to private practice, he could amass a fortune
rapidly. As it is, he has many cases forced upon him,

especially difficult cases of surgery. If a Turkish Pacha breaks his bones, he will have no one to set them right but the American missionary. But Dr. Post prefers to give his services to the poor, and of these services there is no end. Every man who gets into a street fight, and is battered and bruised, feels that he has a right to call on him for help. One morning we were riding out of the yard, when we met several men coming in, one of whom was bleeding fearfully. The doctor sprang out in an instant, and calling for a pail of water, washed the poor fellow's head till he discovered that the injuries were not fatal, prescribed for him on the spot, told his friends how to bind up his wound, wrote an order on the dispensary for the medicines which he needed, and springing into his buggy again, was off to some other duty. This sort of thing is of frequent occurrence. He is going from morning till night, giving his services in the Hospital without any compensation, as well as his lectures in the College, writing books and editing a medical journal. He has prepared a series of Text Books on Surgery, Materia Medica, Botany, Zoology, and Physiology, besides a Concordance of the Arabic Bible, a large octavo volume. Then for want of sufficient occupation, to fill up the time he edits a Monthly Medical Journal, which he has carried on his shoulders for years. /

To complete the work of the College, was added to it some ten years ago a Theological Department, a legacy from that sainted man, who in his mountain home upon Lebanon, used to prepare young men for the ministry. When at last, worn down with labor, he left for America to die, that course of instruction was removed to Beirut, and made a Department of the College. It is now under the care of Rev. Dr. Dennis, a man whose thorough scholarly training at Princeton, and many qualifications both of mind and heart, eminently fit him for the work of educating young men. In the instruction he is aided in different portions of the course of study by Drs. Van Dyck and Eddy, men of long experience, who, having been themselves greatly useful in the Church, know how to teach others to be useful also. With such equipments, and growing in strength every year, this Protestant College is an immeasurable good to the country. /

/ Such are the monuments of a power which is better than ships and guns. If asked what America has to show in the East, we answer, No battle-fields like those of the Crimea, no siege of Sebastopol, no bombardment of Alexandria ; but on the Bosphorus there stands a College founded by American liberality, which is as eloquent in one way as the cemetery at Scutari, which contains so many of the noble English dead, is in another. That College will do more, in the ages to come, for the regeneration of Turkey, than was wrought by all the fearful sacrifice of life, the sad memorial of which is in that hallowed ground where sleep "the unreturning brave." What Robert College is to European Turkey, the College at Beirut is to Syria. /

Our visit is coming to a close. We have made the tour of the Holy Land, and in leaving it, our reflections are of a mingled character : sorrow and pain alternating with love and tenderness. Sometimes we have been moved to a feeling of contempt. In riding over its rugged hills, I have asked myself again and again, Can this be the Promised Land?—and inwardly thanked God that it was not the land promised to our fathers. Old Massachusetts is worth a hundred Palestines. In that Commonwealth which we are proud to call our mother, there is more intelligence, more wealth and comfort, more domestic virtue and happiness, more order and civilization, yes, and more genuine

Christianity, than in all the land of the East. But let us not be lifted up with pride, because of our prosperity, and say boastingly, "He hath not dealt so with any people"; nor look with a pity but little removed from scorn on those whose house is left unto them desolate. Rather would we come with the Jews to their wailing-place, by the foundation stones of the Temple, and cry "O God, the heathen are come into thine inheritance," and pray that after all these ages the time to favor Zion may come. Let us not forget that this land, so bleak and barren now, has given Christ to the world ; that it is the cradle of our Religion ; and that but for it, the Commonwealth of Old England and the Commonwealths of New England would never have been born. Of all that we have, not of Religion only, but of Liberty also, we must trace back the origin to the Galilean Hills. /

At length the end must come ; the farewells must be spoken. As we sat round the table for the last time, with Dean Howson for a guest, our hearts were divided between the land where we had enjoyed so much in wandering among its holy hills, and the dear homes of England and America ; after which Dr. Post and Dr. Dennis " accompanied me to the ship," a steamer of the Austrian Lloyds, which was crowded with passengers, among whom were many English and American clergymen, who having been to Jerusalem for the Holy Week, and made the tour of Palestine, were now taking their departure from the East. The day was nearly gone when the ship turned her head to the west, and bore away for Cyprus. Slowly came down over the sea the soft Eastern twilight, in which we lingered, gazing at the receding shores, till they grew dim in the gathering darkness, and the last glow of sunset faded from the top of Lebanon. /

## Dr. FIELD'S TRAVELS ROUND THE WORLD.

### I.

# FROM THE LAKES OF KILLARNEY TO THE GOLDEN HORN.

## CHARLES SCRIBNER'S SONS, Publishers.

743 AND 745 Broadway, New York.

## II.

# FROM EGYPT TO JAPAN.

### From the NEW YORK OBSERVER.

" The present volume comprises by far the most novel, romantic, and interesting part of the Journey (Round the World), and the story of it is told and the scenes are painted by the hand of a master of the pen.  Dr. Field is a veteran traveller ; he knows well what to see, and (which is still more important to the reader) he knows well what to describe and how to do it."

### From Prof. ROSWELL D. HITCHCOCK, D.D., LL.D.

" In this second volume, Dr. Field, I think, has surpassed himself in the first, and this is saying a good deal.   In both volumes the editorial instinct and habit are conspicuous.  Dr. Prime has said that an editor should have six senses, the sixth being, a " sense of the *interesting*."  Dr. Field has this to perfection. * *"

### From the NEW YORK HERALD.

" It would be impossible by extracts to convey an adequate idea of the abundance, or picturesque freshness of these sketches of travel, without copying a large part of the book."

### From Rev. Dr. R. S. STORRS.

" It is indeed a charming book—full of fresh information, picturesque description, and thoughtful studies of men, countries, and civilizations."

### From Rev. Dr. A. P. PEABODY, late editor of the North American Review.

" I have never, within anything like the same space, seen so much said of Egypt, or so wisely or so well.   Much as I have read about Egypt—many volumes indeed—I have found some of these descriptions more graphic, more realistic, than I have ever met or expect to meet elsewhere."

### By CHARLES DUDLEY WARNER, in the Hartford Courant.

" It is thoroughly entertaining ; the reader's interest is never allowed to flag : the author carries us forward from land to land with uncommon vivacity, enlivens the way with a good humor, a careful observation, and treats all people with a refreshing liberality."

*One Vol., Crown 8vo.  Price, $2.00.*

## CHARLES SCRIBNER'S SONS, Publishers,

### 743 and 745 Broadway, New York.

# ON THE DESERT.

### WITH A BRIEF REVIEW OF RECENT EVENTS IN EGYPT.

An account of a journey in the track of the Israelites along the Red Sea among the peaks of Sinai, through the Desert of the Wandering, and up to the Promised Land.

### From Dr. HOWARD CROSBY.

"No books of travel have ever so fascinated me as those of Dr. H. M. Field."

### From Canon FARRAR, Westminster Abbey.

"I found it so interesting that I could not lay it down till I had finished it."

### From NOAH SWAYNE, LL.D., late Justice of the Supreme Court of the United States.

"Although I had been over the same ground before with Dean Stanley and others, I find the work extremely interesting."

### From Rev. W. G. T. SHEDD, D.D.

"I see the desert and the mountains, and the Arabs, and the camels, and all the strange scenery, without the toil, heat, and danger."

### From Rev. T. W. CHAMBERS, D.D., of New York, who made the journey across the Desert to Mount Sinai in 1867,

"Those who have been over the ground will bear witness to the author's literal accuracy. The reader will get a better idea of the real characteristics of the Sinaitic Desert and its inhabitants from these pages, than from any other accessible volume."

### From the NEW YORK HERALD.

"There is not an uninteresting chapter in the book. It is entertaining throughout. It depicts men and countries in a picturesque and thoughtful manner, and is likely to meet with as much favor as the author's former capital books of travel."

*One Vol., Crown 8vo.   Price, $2.00.*

## CHARLES SCRIBNER'S SONS, Publishers,

743 AND 745 BROADWAY, NEW YORK.

www.ingramcontent.com/pod-product-compliance
Lightning Source LLC
Chambersburg PA
CBHW030401270326
41926CB00009B/1219